LOOKING BACK AT BRITAIN

DEPRESSION YEARS

1930s

DEPRESSION YEARS

1930s

Brian Moynahan

 Reader's Digest | gettyimages

CONTENTS

1930s IMAGE GALLERY

FRONT COVER: The Jarrow Marchers walk through a town in northeast England in October 1936, shortly after setting off on their long trek to London to petition Parliament for action on unemployment and poverty.

BACK COVER: A stuntman takes off in a customised mini-plane at Alexandra Palace, London, in 1930.

TITLE PAGE: The rudder of the SS *Arctees*, a ship launched in 1934 from the yard of the Furness Shipbuilding Co, Haverton-on-Tees, County Durham. The *Arctees* was designed by Sir Joseph Isherwood following his new 'Arcform' hull design, intended to improve fuel consumption.

OPPOSITE: Two young women enjoying themselves on a ride at Southend. The photograph, by Kurt Hutton, was originally published in the Picture Post in 1938.

FOLLOWING PAGES:

A parade of bathing beauties at the open air swimming pool in Blackpool in August 1936.

Crowds in Trafalgar Square catch a fleeting – and badly focused – glimpse of George VI's coronation procession through periscope viewers on 12 May, 1937.

British women practise their marksmanship at the start of the war in this image taken for Life magazine by William Vandivert, a colleague of the famous war photographer, Robert Capa.

Boys from Bradford line up for a dose of medicine while on holiday in the seaside resort of Morecambe in May 1939.

FROM HIGH
TO **LOW**

This was the great age of the air adventurer, and the decade opened in hope and glory. The public imagination was transfixed above all by the 'aviatrix', the plucky girl flyer piloting her flimsy biplane alone across oceans and deserts. And Britain had her very own air adventuress: Amy Johnson from Kingston upon Hull. Slight, slender and beautiful, she was the brave and battling heroine who kept spirits up as the Depression began to bite deep in the early Thirties.

PUTTING BRITAIN FIRST Amy Johnson sticking 'Buy British' posters on her aircraft in 1931. Protectionism flew in the face of Britain's long advocacy of free trade and invited foreign retaliation, but to many it seemed the only answer to the lengthening dole queues.

ADVENTURES IN THE AIR

On 5 May, 1930, Amy Johnson took off from Croydon, then London's major airport, for the 11,000-mile flight to Australia. She was 27 years old and alone at the controls of a second-hand de Havilland Gypsy Moth biplane that her father had helped her to buy. The plane was named 'Jason' after the trademark of her father's fisheries company in Hull. Nineteen and a half days later, Johnson landed at Darwin in northern Australia. In recognition of the achievement, she was awarded a CBE at home, while the Australians honoured her by giving her their No 1 civil pilot's licence. Her aircraft was preserved at the Science Museum in Kensington. The public loved her. They sang:

> 'Amy, wonderful Amy
> How can you blame me
> For loving you?'

'AMY, WONDERFUL AMY'
The public adored Amy Johnson, and it is easy to see why. She was courageous, down-to-earth and not afraid to get her hands dirty. She was the world's first fully qualified female aircraft mechanic. She poses happily here in her oil-stained overalls, while working on the engine of her de Havilland Gypsy Moth, a single-engine, wood-and-fabric biplane with an open cockpit. The photograph was taken in March 1930. A few weeks later, she was smashing the England to Australia flying record. On her return, an estimated million people lined the route from Croydon to London to welcome her home.

Giants of the skies

The pilots of heavier-than-air machines were the heroes and heroines of the day, but it was thought that the future of commercial passenger flight lay in huge airships, rather than frail and tiny aeroplanes like Amy's. The huge, gas-filled bodies were not fast, but they carried passenger compartments beneath them that were spacious and lavish enough to have grand pianos and dining areas, and to carry passengers in style. Here, too, the British were pioneers. The British Empire covered a quarter of the land surface of the planet, and 'Imperial air routes' were planned to stitch it together. A few months after Amy's successful solo venture, an airship proving flight was planned.

The giant R101 set out from its base at Cardington, Bedfordshire, at 7pm on a Saturday in October 1930. The airship was already famous. It had cruised over London – the press described it as 'large as the *Mauritania*', the famous ocean liner – and its sister ship the R100 had flown across the Atlantic to Canada. This time the destination was India, with senior men of the Air Ministry on board, including Lord Thompson, the air minister. A few hours after taking off the airship flew into a violent rainstorm near Beauvais, 40 miles from Paris. Low-lying cloud prevented the captain, Flight Lieutenant Irwin, from flying at altitude.

DOOMED GIANT

The R101 in its hangar at Cardington in Bedfordshire in 1930. Airships were thought well-proven by now. The Admiralty had built two hydrogen-powered airships on the lines of the German Zeppelins after the war. The R34 crossed the Atlantic to Long Island safely in 1919. The first man to arrive in America by air from Britain was a Major Pritchard, who leaped from the airship by parachute to give instructions to the ground-crew. A stowaway was found in the gas bags. The trip took 108 hours, but it was still hoped that airships were the future of commercial flying. The R100 and R101 were luxury craft. Here (right) waiters serve members of a Dominions Conference at smartly laid tables in the dining room of R101. The R100 made a successful flight to Canada in 1930 and it was hoped that the R101, which had some structural alterations made to her, would prove even more triumphant on her test flight to India.

The mass of rainwater on top of the gigantic flight envelope forced the airship lower, then gusting winds appear to have damaged the nose, pushing the ship into a steep dive. From the control room Irwin ordered all engines to slow, trying to effect a safe emergency landing. At 2am, the R101 hit the ground.

Although the impact was gentle – as witnessed by the ship's remarkably intact skeleton (below) – the hydrogen gas bags exploded and flames enveloped the passenger gondola below the airship. Only eight men, all of them crew, survived. Among them was the wireless operator, who telephoned the news to the Air Ministry from Beauvais. Forty-eight passengers and crew, including Lord Thompson, were burned to death. The Sunday newspapers in Britain printed special editions during the day. The French declared a day of national mourning.

Two days later there was a bizarre twist to the story. The National Laboratory for Psychical Research had been founded in 1925 to carry out examination of psychical phenomena and the director was investigating the powers of a trance medium called Mrs Garrett. During the session, she began relaying messages from Flight Lieutenant Irwin who had died in the R101 crash. He was said to have complained through her that the engine capacity had not been increased when the airship was enlarged, so the ship was underpowered. He also said the gas-bags had been leaking, and there had not been enough trials. These points were later confirmed by the official enquiry, which found that the immediate cause of the disaster was gradual loss of gas through holes worn in the gas-bags.

The destruction of the R101, which had cost £500,000 to build, then a huge sum, put paid to the hopes of Britain developing regular intercontinental airship passenger services. The Air Ministry stopped building the craft, the R100 was dismantled and the base at Cardington was closed. It was an omen, not just for travel by airship, but for the high hopes for the Thirties.

SIFTING THE WRECKAGE
A charred skeleton is all that remained of the R101, which crashed in the very early hours of 5 October, 1930. Its destination had been Karachi in what was then still India, but the airship got no further than Beauvais in northern France before the buffeting of wind and the weight of heavy rain forced it to crash land. The hydrogen in the giant body of the ship caught fire and most of those on board were burned to death, including the government air minister and many of Britain's airship experts. The coffins of the victims were brought from France to Westminster Abbey amid an outpouring of what Malcolm Muggeridge called 'verbose grief'. The crash marked the end of airship development in Britain.

IN ECONOMIC MELTDOWN

'I say with all the seriousness I can command that the national position is so grave', announced Philip Snowden, the chancellor of the exchequer, in his long-winded style, 'that drastic and disagreeable measures will have to be taken if budgetary equilibrium is to be maintained.' What he meant was that the economic crisis was so deep that harsh medicine was needed. Snowden – seen here with his wife in happier days, leaving the Labour Party Conference at Brighton in October 1929 – was a no-nonsense Yorkshireman, said to have coined the phrase 'the idle rich'. He was an orthodox chancellor, who believed in free trade and balanced budgets. He had no answer to the emergency he now faced. The failure of Kreditanstalt in Austria was followed by other banking collapses on the Continent. Then a report that the UK's budget deficit would reach £120 million panicked investors, and money began haemorrhaging from London and sterling. The Bank of England borrowed from France and America to staunch the flow, but to no avail. By 31 August, 1931, the situation had become so bad that a National Government was formed. Ramsay MacDonald remained as Prime Minister and for a while it seemed his finest hour – 'money was saved, England was saved'. The new government won a sweeping mandate in a general election on 6 October to prescribe stiff doses of economic medicine to the country. A triumphant MacDonald savoured the moment (below). But the bulk of the Labour Party and many Liberals refused to follow their leaders, and MacDonald was reviled as a traitor clinging to power on the coat-tails of the dominant Conservatives.

It was clear that the British economy was in deepening crisis. It was not simply prestige projects like airships whose day was done. Deep, across-the-board cuts in public spending were looming closer. The first casualty was the Labour government of Ramsay MacDonald. When it had come to power, in June 1929, the number of registered unemployed stood at 1,163,000, or a little under 10 per cent of the workforce. By June 1930, as the effects of the Wall Street Crash of October 1929 rippled out across the world, the number had risen to almost 2 million. At the end of 1930 it hit 2.5 million. The position of the working man was now more perilous than at any stage since the end of the Napoleonic wars.

It did not help that MacDonald was trying to run a minority government. Labour had actually won fewer votes than the Conservatives in the 1929 general election. They had more seats – 287 to the Tories' 260 – but not an overall majority. The balance was held by 59 Liberal MPs. During the election campaign Labour had made an 'unqualified pledge' to deal with unemployment, and as the jobless numbers snowballed, it became a huge embarrassment. MacDonald and his Chancellor of the Exchequer, Philip Snowden, had no solution to the abyss.

Part of the problem lay with the Prime Minister himself. MacDonald, tall and good-looking, had risen from lowly beginnings as the son of a Scottish ploughman and a servant girl. He had been born illegitimate, a source of shame at a time when only two or three in a hundred were born out of wedlock; it was rumoured that he was actually the son of a marquis. He was tough and durable – he lived on water and oatmeal when he first came to London – and he was a fine speaker, with rolling Scottish 'Rs' and a messianic gleam in his eye.

In 1930 MacDonald was heading his second Labour government, but his best days politically were already behind him. The Socialist beliefs that had driven him had dissipated. A former admirer said of him that 'he does not believe in the creed we have always preached'. He was touchy, intolerant and hated criticism. He had little grasp of economics. 'Unemployment is baffling us. The simple fact is that our population is too great for our trade', he wrote in his journal. 'I sit in my room in Downing Street alone and in silence. The cup has been put to my lips – and it is empty.' He still delivered speeches with panache, but at times was almost incoherent. 'My head won't work', he said.

Unemployment was equally baffling to the minister in charge of it, Jimmy Thomas, the former boss of the railwaymen's union. Thomas made much of being a man of the people – wags said that he dropped his aitches with as much care as a woman applying make-up – and he was frantic at his powerlessness to

FRUSTRATION ON THE STREETS
Communist demonstrators come up against police at Tower Hill in London during a rally to protest against joblessness in March 1930. Fears spread that mass unemployment would boost extremists, but in fact the country remained remarkably stable and moderate. No doubt it helped that, unlike Germany, the Great War had ended in victory in 1918 and not humiliation, and that people's savings had not been wiped out by rampant inflation. But the general conduct of the British public during times of hardship also showed that respect for Parliament and the rule of law had deep roots.

help them in such hard times. A Cabinet colleague, Arthur Henderson, said that Thomas was 'completely rattled and in such a state of panic that he is bordering on lunacy…'. A sense of drift ate into the Labour Cabinet. Its brightest young star, Sir Oswald Mosley, walked out of it to found his own New Party.

Meanwhile, another new party had been founded by two press barons. In 1930 Canadian-born Lord Beaverbrook had started an 'Empire free trade crusade'. His flagship paper, the *Daily Express*, began to print a small crusader next to the title on the front page – it still carries it today. Beaverbrook wanted a tariff put on all goods coming into Britain, with preference for those coming from the empire. *Express* editorials attacked the principles of free trade as Victorian and outdated. Lord Rothermere, owner of the *Daily Mail*, agreed and cooperated with Beaverbrook in founding the United Empire Party. A quarter of a million readers contributed £100,000 to the party's funds. Predictably, the two moguls fell out; they backed rival candidates at a by-election in Paddington in October 1930. The seat was won by Beaverbrook's Empire Crusader, Vice Admiral Taylor. Another Crusader was elected for Islington East, but this was the party's high point.

Shaken to the core

By the early summer of 1931, the government was deep in crisis. The trade unions were antagonistic. The radical left-wing MPs of the Independent Labour Party, though nominally allies, were in more or less permanent rebellion. The morale of the Parliamentary Labour Party (PLP) was in tatters. The agreement with the Liberals, on whose votes the government depended, was beginning to splinter. Dismal by-election results added to the gloom. As if in physical reflection of the

STRIKING TO NO AVAIL
In the worst-hit industries – shipbuilding and shipping, iron and steel, coal, textiles, heavy engineering – whole communities were laid waste. At first, many workers believed industrial action might help. Here (top left), striking shipyard workers gather outside the offices of the TGWU in Tooley

Street, London, in May 1930. Earlier that year, the miners above staged an underground 'sit-in' at their colliery in the North over pay and conditions; here, they are seen leaving, their eyes shielded by visors against the unaccustomed daylight.

The worst year for strikes was 1931 with 6.9 million days lost; 1932 was little better, with 6.4 million. By 1934 industrial action had abated and fewer than 1 million days were lost to strikes that year. Though there was an upsurge in 1937, the great crisis in labour relations had passed.

The suffering in mining communities in the Thirties was acute. In its heyday, coal-mining employed 1.2 million men, but by 1931 two-thirds of men in some pit villages were without work. More than 40 per cent of miners were out of work in 1932 – the number was much higher in the inland valleys of Wales, in Merthyr, Rhondda and Aberdare. Even by 1935, when the worst of the depression had lifted in other sectors, a third of miners were still left idle.

STORMY WEATHER
Scarborough reflected the national condition all too well when this photograph was taken in August 1931: storm-tossed, sunless, cold and bleak. The epicentre of the Dogger Bank earthquake two months before had been 60 miles off the Yorkshire coast and many coastal towns experienced damage. In Filey, Scarborough's near neighbour, the tremor twisted a church spire. Yorkshire and the North were hard hit by the economic crisis, but enough money was still being made for the genteel tea rooms and hotels of resorts like Scarborough to survive without too much fuss. In November 1933, J B Priestley visited Blackpool, the largest of the resorts, and found that the 'great roaring spangled beast is hibernating', but it was back in business with a vengeance by Christmas.

shaky state of the country, the Dogger Bank earthquake of June 1931 – the largest ever in Britain, measuring 6.1 on the Richter scale – was felt across the land.

The public finances were caught in a vicious circle. In 1931, tax yields fell by almost a third from their 1928 level, while the cost of unemployment benefit soared from £12 million to £125 million. Exports halved in value. The £40 million government deficit was expected to double in 1932. The collapse of the Austrian bank Kreditanstalt sparked bank collapses in Germany and hit the City of London, which had large loans to Germany. Foreign creditors, mainly French, sold sterling. In less than a month the Bank of England was down £60 million in bullion and foreign exchange reserves. Before leaving for America on holiday, Montagu Norman, governor of the Bank of England, said that ration books should be printed 'in case the currency collapsed and the country had to revert to barter'.

Bankers warned that sterling would fall off the precipice unless confidence was restored by a more balanced budget. Snowden pressed Cabinet colleagues for cuts. On 31 July, the day Parliament rose for the summer recess, he tried to hustle them into agreement: he released a report, without comment or warning, that predicted a budget deficit of £120 million by the following spring and recommended spending cuts of £96 million, including a 10 per cent cut in the dole.

Snowden's aim was to soften up opinion in Britain to accept drastic action, but instead the run on the pound got worse as fears abroad intensified. Ministers were called back from holiday and on 21 August agreed to £56 million in cuts, mainly from public sector salaries, against vigorous TUC protests. But even this was so far short of the recommended £96 million that it failed to prop up sterling. Two days later, the Labour Cabinet voted 11 to 9 for the cut in unemployment benefit, but the dissenting minority – including Arthur Henderson, Foreign Secretary and Labour Party General Secretary – was too large to ignore. Believing it to be the end of his government, MacDonald came out of the bad-tempered meeting and said: 'I'm going off to the Palace to throw in my hand.'

'... as near a broken man as I have seen in a big job ... The fizz is out of him. He hasn't a bone in his body. It is all pulp. His difficulties are almost overwhelming.'

Lloyd George speaking of Prime Minister Ramsay MacDonald in 1931

Forming a national coalition

When MacDonald arrived at the Palace, King George V gave him some good advice. He suggested that MacDonald remain as Prime Minister, at the head of a new National Government. MacDonald was happy to be persuaded to stay, for by now he was as addicted to the fruits and trappings of high office as George V was to shooting and stamp-collecting.

The next day, 24 August, 1931, MacDonald was back at the Palace to tell the King that Stanley Baldwin, the Conservative leader and a former prime minister, had agreed to serve under him in a new National Government. It was, Baldwin said, 'for a limited period. There is no question of a permanent coalition.' But in fact that is precisely what happened. Britain would have a national coalition government until 1945. Four Conservatives joined MacDonald's 10-man Cabinet,

THE COALITION CABINET

A small crowd gathers at the gates of Downing Street on 24 August, 1931, waiting for news at the height of the government crisis (left). The next day, cabinet ministers of the new and as yet unelected National Government were photographed in the garden of Number 10 (right). They are, standing left to right: C Lister; Jimmy Thomas, Dominions Secretary; Rufus Isaacs, Marquis of Reading, Foreign Secretary (albeit briefly); Neville Chamberlain, soon to be Conservative Chancellor of the Exchequer; and Sir Samuel Hoare, Viscount Templewood, Conservative Secretary of State for India. Seated, left to right: Philip Snowden; the Conservative leader Stanley Baldwin, Lord President of the Council; Prime Minister Ramsay MacDonald; Herbert Samuel, the Liberal Home Secretary; and Lord Stanley, Parliamentary and Financial Secretary to the Admiralty.

When free trade was dropped, and Imperial Preference brought in by the Ottawa Agreements of February 1932, Snowden and Herbert Samuel both resigned. Neville Chamberlain, the coming man, said that Ottawa was 'the crowning achievement in a year wonderful with endeavour'. Preference for Empire goods was followed by 'most-favoured nation' trade treaties with Argentina and the Scandinavian countries. Marketing boards were set up for milk, potatoes and hops, while British wheat was guaranteed a share of the market. It was remarkable that this huge extension of State control was largely Conservative-inspired.

including Baldwin and Neville Chamberlain, soon to replace Snowden as Chancellor. Most Labour MPs passed into opposition. The split was bitter and long-lasting. MacDonald and the few who remained with him – Snowden and Jimmy Thomas, the former railwayman now Dominions Secretary – were reviled as Tory lackeys and expelled from the party. For good measure, Thomas was also thrown out of the National Union of Railwaymen.

Pay cuts all round

On 9 September, 1931, Snowden announced salary cuts of 10 per cent for all government employees. Savings of £25 million were to be made in unemployment benefit: a single man's dole fell from 17 shillings a week to 15s 3d. Labour MPs attacked their erstwhile colleague as a Scrooge, he called them Bolsheviks. The King volunteered for a cut in the Civil List payment he received from £470,000 to £430,000. The Prince of Wales presented the Exchequer with £10,000 from his £65,000 income from the Duchy of Cornwall. The American philanthropist Edward Harkness gave £2 million to be spent 'for the benefit of Great Britain'.

The Admiralty now announced pay cuts across the board for all ranks in the Navy. For officers, the cuts equated to around 10 per cent, but for many lower ratings – and therefore the lowest paid – the cut was equivalent to having their pay docked by 25 per cent. Jolly Jack Tar was understandably upset. On 14 September, some sailors of the Atlantic Fleet at Invergordon refused to obey orders. Some of the world's most powerful warships were lying at anchor off the small town on the Moray Firth, including the battleships *Rodney* and *Nelson*, whose 16-inch guns could throw a one-ton shell for 20 miles. At 6am on 15 September, they refused to put to sea for exercises. There was loose talk of training the big guns on Ramsay MacDonald's house at nearby Lossiemouth.

This was by no means a full-blooded mutiny – the men still stood to attention when Marine bands played 'God Save The King'. The only coherent demands were in a 'loyal manifesto' dictated by Len Wincott, a seaman aboard the cruiser *Norfolk*, which beseeched the Admiralty to 'amend the drastic cuts in pay which

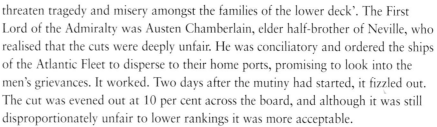

threaten tragedy and misery amongst the families of the lower deck'. The First Lord of the Admiralty was Austen Chamberlain, elder half-brother of Neville, who realised that the cuts were deeply unfair. He was conciliatory and ordered the ships of the Atlantic Fleet to disperse to their home ports, promising to look into the men's grievances. It worked. Two days after the mutiny had started, it fizzled out. The cut was evened out at 10 per cent across the board, and although it was still disproportionately unfair to lower rankings it was more acceptable.

The only other group to have a pay cut restored – this time in full – were the judges. Sir William Holdsworth, a flamboyantly moustachioed professor of English law at Oxford, argued that it was wrong for judges to suffer because they had to try cases which 'involve enormous amounts of money'. Since a 'wrong decision may inflict on a litigant the unmerited sacrifice of a sum which vastly exceeds the annual savings on all judicial salaries', it was wrong to expose judges to the same cuts as other civil servants. The logic was astounding and utterly self-serving – no lawyer argued that the pay of a battleship's captain should not be touched, because of the calamity that could result from his error of judgment – but judges had their full salaries restored nonetheless. Anger at this intensified when it was revealed that an Attorney General could make £45,000 a year. At the same time, a letter-writer to *The Times* thought it 'sinister' that a family of five were reported to get 'no less than 69 shillings a week' (not quite £3.50) in unemployment benefit. The rich welcomed the Means Test as a way of dealing with such 'outrage'.

Another Admiralty bungle

The judges got away with it, but the Admiralty got it wrong again, with disastrous consequences. Despite a promise of no reprisals following the settlement brokered by Chamberlain, it dismissed 24 ratings as ringleaders and inflicted punishment gunnery drills on others. Worst of all, it tried to hush up the incident. Seamen like Fred Copeman, an idealist who later fought with the International Brigades in Spain, were not to be silenced. News got out. The press, denied a proper briefing, blew the whole incident up as a full-scale mutiny.

Mutiny had unthinkable consequences. The Royal Navy was the symbol of British might across the world, keeping the sea lanes open to the empire. Foreign newspapers splashed the story across front pages. Britain, they claimed, was on the verge of mutiny. Investors took panic again and another £43 million flooded abroad in less than four days. The pound could not withstand such pressure.

Abandoning the gold standard

Gold was the internationally accepted means of exchange, but the strains of the slump had made sterling grossly over-valued in relation to gold – and the markets knew it. The National Government bowed to the inevitable. Britain came off the gold standard on 21 September, 1931.

NAVAL ACTION
Cadets doing PT on the deck of the Royal Navy battleship HMS *Ramillies*. What began in the Fleet at Invergordon as an angry protest against the Admiralty's proposed pay cut would end with the government being forced to suspend sterling from the gold standard. Having bungled the pay cut, the Admiralty made matters worse by trying to hush up news of the sailors' refusal to put to sea. It trickled out, of course, and was blazoned as a full-scale mutiny by the press at home and abroad. Gold poured out of London once more and sterling tottered. The pound found its new value at around 70 per cent of its old gold-backed value.

On the placards: "23 CUTS IN 10 YEARS IS THIS EQUAL SACRIFICE?", "23 CUTS SINCE 1921 IS CALLED EQUALITY", "WHAT ABOUT THE RENTS", "WORKERS OF THE WORLD UNITE"

JUSTICE AND EQUALITY?

The statue of Lady Justice, by sculptor F W Pomeroy, gets a wash and brush-up above the Central Criminal Court in Old Bailey, London. Justice was in a less happy state of repair in several countries on the Continent. It had been crushed by Mussolini's dictatorship in Italy and by Stalin in the Soviet Union, and it was under increasing assault in Germany and Spain. At home, the concern was more with pay cuts and unemployment, which was threatening even those with supposedly secure jobs. This long line of protestors (above) are civil servants – some 20,000 of them – marching down Piccadilly in London in 1931. One of them holds aloft a banner bearing the Marxist slogan, 'Workers of the World Unite'.

It was a huge shock. According to the writer Alec Waugh: '"Safe as the Rock of Gibraltar" and "Safe as the Bank of England" had been the two pillars that sustained our way of life. Now one of them was gone.' It was forbidden to take gold out of the country for six months. The 1925 Act which required the sale of gold at a fixed price was suspended. The price could float and find its own daily level. The bank rate – the rate of interest on loans – was raised from 4½ per cent to 6 per cent. The stock exchange closed for the day to enable brokers and jobbers to adjust. The public were assured that, as one headline put it, there was 'No Need For Alarm'. But it was the final evidence for Britain's wealthier classes, if any were needed, that the good life of the Twenties was over.

Sterling fell by about 30 per cent and the effect was felt immediately in hotels and resorts across the South of France, the Tyrol, Switzerland and Italy. They were left half-empty as the newly impoverished British came home. Soon, foreign travel was said to be unpatriotic. Cruises, where sunshine was priced in pounds, soared in popularity. Nerves were calmed in October by Noël Coward's *Cavalcade*, a sentimental celebration of things British – the Boer War, Mafeking, stiff upper lips on the *Titanic* and in the Great War – threaded together by a string of popular songs. The show ends on a high patriotic note as a decadent nightclub blues is drowned out by a soaring 'God Save the King' sung by the whole cast. The royal family attended the second night, and the *Daily Mail* serialised it.

National landslide

Two weeks later, in October 1931, the National Government went to the country. It felt it needed a 'doctor's mandate' from the people to deal with the economic sickness. The election was a disaster for the Labour Party, which was woefully ill-prepared, its policies vague, impractical and over-optimistic: 'Bolshevism run

mad', said the 'traitor' Jimmy Thomas. Most of the party's pamphlets and posters had to be shredded because they bore the name or picture of the 'arch-traitor' himself, Ramsay MacDonald. The ones they did run made great play of the Invergordon incident. They carried a picture of the wartime battle of Jutland. The Royal Navy, it said, had thrashed the German Kaiser then, and it had now beaten Montague Norman, the governor of the Bank of England.

The Tory press branded this an insult to the Navy, but it need not have worried. The voters approved, massively, of National candidates, electing 554 of them. All of Baldwin's Conservatives ran on National tickets, and 470 were rewarded with seats. Only 46 Labour MPs and a rump of 16 Liberal rebels were elected. The new Cabinet had 20 members. MacDonald remained Prime Minister, with three other National Labour ministers. Sir John Simon, one of five Liberals, became Foreign Secretary. But the real power – and all the key economic posts apart from the Board of Trade – lay with Stanley Baldwin and the 10 other Tories.

Yet another financial crisis followed the suicide of the Swedish 'match magnate', Ivar Krueger. In March 1932, he shot himself through the heart in his Paris apartment. Stock markets round the world tumbled further. Sympathy for him waned when it was found that he owed £50 million, and that he had forged 42 Italian Treasury Bonds, with a face value of £500,000 each, in an attempt to prop up his ailing fortune.

THE ELECTION TRAIL
Ramsay MacDonald campaigning for his new National Government among the mining communities of Co Durham. This photograph was taken at Haswell Plough, near Seaham, on 13 October, 1931 – his 65th birthday. The Liberal Party tried to woo women voters (top), while the government clearly intended to win over Labour voters with this poster (above). In the event the coalition National Government won votes right across the political spectrum and returned to Parliament with a huge majority.

SPRINGS OF HOPE

There was no doubt that the British were less religious than they had been and that fewer went to church than in their parents' generation. In York, for example, Sunday attendance had fallen from 35.5 per cent of people in 1901 to just 17 per cent in 1935. The traditional church-going 'Sabbath' had turned into the 'weekend', a time for gardening, hobbies, sports and rambles more than prayer. Nonconformists, pillars of the Liberals, declined as much as their party in their old heartlands in Wales, Cornwall and the West Midlands.

But even though society had grown more secular, public morals were still subject to old standards. Attitudes remained strongly against divorce, artificial birth control, obscenity, alcohol, homosexuality and the 'Continental Sunday' characterised by the opening of libraries, galleries and museums. No first class cricket or football was played on Sundays. Pubs remained firmly shut in parts of Wales and Scotland. Parliament was opened by prayers. The crowd at the Cup Final sang the hymn 'Abide With Me'. Prayers were said each day in schools, prisons, law courts, on warships and in the army. Britain was still a consciously Christian country: every child knew the Lord's Prayer and a carol or two.

The Church remained a powerful influence – somewhat to everyone's surprise. A new cathedral for Guildford was designed by Edward Maufe in 1932. Some traditions were being relaxed: existing cathedrals followed Canterbury in opening for visitors between services on Sunday, and women were allowed in without hats. T S Eliot's new play *Murder in the Cathedral* caused a sensation at the Canterbury festival. It portrayed the killing by four knights of Thomas Becket in 1170, after Henry II had muttered that he wished to be rid of 'this turbulent priest'.

Piety was left largely to nonconformists and Scots puritans. People went to Anglican services from habit, for the singing, to hear local gossip, and as a preliminary to a Sunday session in the pub – 'thirst after righteousness' – as much as for worship. In 1931, though, William Temple, then the archbishop of York, led a week's mission to Oxford. It had a huge impact. On the final evening, a packed audience joined Temple to sing 'When I survey the wondrous Cross'. After the first verse, the archbishop stopped the singing and said the next verse had 'tremendous words'. If the congregation believed the words to the bottom of their souls, they should sing them as passionately as they could. If they didn't mean them, they should stay silent. 'If you mean them even a little', he said, 'and want them to mean them more, sing them very softly.' It was brilliant theatre. They looked at Isaac Watt's words on their hymn sheets:

'Were the whole world of nature mine,
That were an offering far too small
Love so amazing, so divine
Demands my soul, my life, my all.'

To hear these words whispered by two thousand young men and women, one of them recalled, was 'an experience never to be erased from my memory till the whole tablet is blotted'. The vicar of the university church believed the Oxford

TOUTING FOR GOLD
Gold became much in demand following the suspension of the gold standard – and there was no shortage of men, like these two in London in 1932, willing to tramp the streets carrying sandwich boards advertising those who were keen to buy. There was a growing fear that paper money might not be worth the paper it was written on, now that it no longer had a guaranteed link to the value of gold.

Mission 'stopped the rot' in Christian life. He thought it was a decisive moment in the history of the young generation, whose effects spread out across the country. It was the moment when 'the tide began to come in', he said, alluding to Matthew Arnold's great Victorian poem on the sea of faith ebbing away. Hope and idealism, it seemed, could still break through the grimness.

In 1932 the Oxford Group, which had been founded by an American evangelist in the Twenties, began to get the attention of popular newspapers. The *Daily Express* ran a series of pieces by young men on the revival in religious feeling. They included 'Bunny' Austin, the tennis champion, who said that he thought Jesus was neither meek nor mild, but 'a man magnificently built, tall and strong' – rather like himself. The Group believed in public confession of sins and gained so many followers that the Albert Hall was hired for their confessionals.

New schools of thought

Experiments were made in 'free' schools – free of discipline rather than fees. The most famous was A S Neill's Summerfields. It specialised in problem children (observers claimed that they were usually the offspring of problem parents) who broke windows, wrote swear words on the walls, played truant and stole. Neill said that he made Summerfields for the children, rather than the other way round. All were free to express their natures to the full without discipline. Neill's proud boast was that he had discovered that children are born sincere, and remain so if they are not warped by conventional education. 'Some turned out sincerely good, a few stayed sincerely bad', Robert Graves wrote. 'Everything got broken.'

Another no-discipline school was run by Bertrand Russell, mathematician, philosopher and advocate of sexual freedom, and his equally libertarian wife, Dora. The Russells thought that the development of 'personality' through free expression was more important than book-learning, which could be picked up later. The problem with this, Graves noted, arose when children went home for the holidays and expressed themselves as they had at school, by swearing or smashing something. They were then 'repressed' or 'disciplined' by irritated neighbours and relatives, if not by the loony parents.

BELIEF IN FRESH AIR
The fad for 'Healthy Living' in the Thirties went as far as open-air lessons, like this one taking place in St James's Park in London. A chill and misty February morning looks anything but healthy for the pupils in their neat caps and blazers, huddled under blankets for warmth, with bottles of milk to keep them going. The figure at the back looks more like an actress in *Wuthering Heights* than a schoolmistress up with the latest educational trends. Dora Russell (right), the feminist and civil libertarian, ran a 'no-discipline school' with her husband Bertrand Russell, the philosopher who had been a vigorous protestor against the Great War. They believed that a child only became 'a whole person' as an adult if allowed freedom of action and expression.

The urge for peace

Peace was in the air in the 1930s, though it was often grounded by brute reality. Peace conferences were held in Montreux, Lausanne, Stresa, Genoa, Rapallo and other pleasant towns, by lake or sea. Each was briefly swamped by delegates, interpreters, stenographers, journalists and photographers, ending with an upbeat final communique – invariably over-optimistic – and the show moved on.

The first World Disarmament Conference was held under the League of Nations banner in Geneva in 1932. It turned into farce. A proposal to ban all bombing from the air was turned down by Sir John Simon, the British Foreign Secretary: the cheapest and most effective way to deal with turbulent tribesmen on India's unruly Northwest Frontier was to send RAF biplanes to bomb them. India was restless. The charismatic nationalist leader Mahatma Gandhi had come to Britain the year before to discuss a new federal constitution. His campaign of 'civil disobedience' and the boycott of British goods was gathering pace in India and concerns for the British Raj were growing. His emaciated body and loin cloth made a stir when he arrived in London, but politically the visit achieved little.

Another proposal at Geneva, to limit tanks to 8 tons, was again rejected by the British, who had 16-ton tanks undergoing trials, and also by the French, who were experimenting with a 60-ton monster. The Soviet Union proposed complete

GREAT SOUL
The visit to London in 1931 of Mahatma Gandhi (right), the Indian independence leader, was not a political success. He had recently been released from a brief prison sentence in India, imposed for defying the unpopular salt monopoly of the British Raj. The dhoti he wore in India was a symbol of his humility and simplicity. In the London rain, though, it looked to some a ridiculous affectation. But there was much goodwill towards him in Britain. Gandhi got a warm welcome away from London, as this photograph with textile workers in Darwen, Lancashire, shows (above). This was generous of them, for a central part of Gandhi's protest against British rule was that India should spin its own cotton, rather than importing cloth made in the mechanised Lancashire mills.

A GALLERY OF PRIZE-WINNERS

British scientists were at the very forefront of new research and development, and throughout the 1930s reaped a host of Nobel prizes in physics, chemistry and physiology and medicine. The three in the top row are among the immortals. Ernest Rutherford (near left, in 1932) was one of 12 children of a wheelwright in New Zealand, and grew up to be one of the greatest pioneers of sub-atomic physics. Scholarships got him to the Cavendish Laboratory at Cambridge, where he discovered three types of uranium radiation. While at Manchester, he won the Nobel prize for chemistry and developed the concept of the 'Rutherford-Bohr atom' of nuclear physics. Becoming Cavendish professor at Cambridge, he predicted the existence of the neutron. Rutherford's colleagues at Cambridge included the Irish physicist Ernest Walton (far left) and John Cockroft (centre), who disintegrated lithium by proton bombardment in 1932. They were jointly awarded the Nobel prize for physics in 1951. Cockroft became the first director of Britain's Atomic Energy Establishment at Harwell in 1946. Other members of the Cavendish team included Patrick Blackett (middle row, far left), who developed a device for studying cosmic radiation, winning a Nobel prize in 1948, and James Chadwick (middle row, centre), who won the Nobel prize for physics in 1935 for discovering the neutron.

Eminent scientists working in other fields included Walter Haworth (middle row, near left), professor of organic chemistry at Birmingham. In 1937 he shared the Nobel prize for chemistry for his work in determining the properties of Vitamin C. The physiologist Henry Hallett Dale (bottom row, far left) worked on the chemical transmission of nerve impulses, winning the 1936 Nobel prize for physiology and medicine with the Austrian Otto Loewi. Dale also discovered acetylcholine. The physiologists Edgar Adrian (bottom row, centre) and Charles Sherrington (near left) shared the Nobel prize for physiology and medicine in 1932 for their work on the function of neurons. Adrian did important research on electrical impulses in the nervous system. He was a pioneer in the study of epilepsy and brain lesions. Sherrington researched reflex action.

disarmament, but this was little more than a propaganda gimmick – it knew that none of the Western capitalist countries would agree.

Students at the Oxford Union showed that pacifism remained strong. They carried a motion in 1933 favouring a refusal to fight for King and Country if called upon to do so. A League of Nations 'peace monarch' was proposed, to reign in Geneva, having been enthroned with due ceremony. Peace campaigners picked names and addresses at random from German telephone directories, and sent them postcards saying that the writer was resolved in all circumstances to practice non-resistance. Dr Maud Royden tried to raise a peace army, whose volunteers would march to the front line in a war and occupy no man's land between the two belligerents, obliging them to call off the war or shoot innocent civilians. It was perhaps as well that this was not put to the test.

Technological strides

It was as well, too, perhaps, that peace activists were not aware of the progress that British scientists were making in controlling and understanding nuclear fission. The team of physicists at the Cavendish Laboratory in Cambridge – James Chadwick, John Cockroft, P M S Blackett and E T S Walton – were leading the world. In 1932, Cockroft and Walton were the first to 'split the atom', causing a nuclear reaction by using artificially accelerated particles. Chadwick discovered the neuron in 1934, confirming that Lord Rutherford had been correct in postulating its existence in 1920. Chadwick also built Britain's first cyclotron in Liverpool in 1935, the same year that he won the Nobel prize for physics.

Cathode ray tubes and electronic cameras were pioneered in Britain by Isaac Shoenberg, director of research at EMI from 1931. EMI and Marconi, another British company, provided the equipment for the world's first regular television service, launched by the BBC from Alexandra Palace in 1936. An offshoot was Radar, the radio location of aircraft. The government gave £10,000 for research into the radar techniques. It proved a bargain in the hands of the brilliant Scottish physicist Robert Watson-Watt. The first radar masts were being built on the Kent and Essex coasts for detecting enemy aircraft in 1936, the year that a Spitfire first flew. Four years later, the combination of fine fighter aircraft and radar to guide them to the squadrons of approaching enemy bombers was to save the nation.

The BBC was the main force in television and radio research. But most developments came from the private sector and the R&D efforts of electronics companies like EMI and Marconi, aircraft builders, engineering firms and chemical giants. Despite the economic problems, investment in research tripled between 1930 and 1938. It was to prove essential to the future war effort, and provided a big pool of scientists and engineers.

Scientists, or 'boffins', were much admired by the public, who soaked up books on astronomy, natural history and geology. Sir James Jeans, an expert in quantum theory and stellar evolution, drew a mass readership for his books on *The Universe* and *The New Background of Science* in 1933. *Mathematics for the Million* and *Science for the Citizen* were bestsellers in 1936 and 1938 for Lancelot Hogben, a professor of zoology. The confidence of scientists was noted by C P Snow, a physicist who also wrote popular novels. In later years he wrote of the Thirties: 'It was difficult to find a scientist who did not believe that the scientific-technological-industrial revolution, accelerating under his eyes, was not doing incomparably more good than harm.'

A NEW AGE OF TECHNOLOGY

The Thirties saw a massive spread of services that we take for granted today. All over the country the infrastructure was being built to ensure that people everywhere could have access to the telephone, to the new wireless programmes broadcast by the BBC and to the benefits of electric power. The developments in radio led to radar, which would prove invaluable when war broke out at the end of the decade.

NEW COMMUNICATIONS Telephone engineers fix telegraph wires to insulators near Staines in Middlesex in 1933. They were employed by the Post Office, since telephone services had evolved from the telegram service: the poles they are working on were still called telegraph poles. Most telephones were now on automatic exchanges and the old upright models, where the user had to juggle with the microphone and a separate earpiece, were being replaced by sleek all-in-one handsets. The lady in the telephone box below – as unmistakably British as red pillar boxes and double-decker buses – is holding one of the new devices. The Post Office was a big employer, and the rise in the number of telephonists in business and the civil service created many new jobs.

The men building a new wireless station near Baldock in Hertfordshire in 1930 (bottom right) were part of a huge expansion that saw most people across the country able to pick up BBC broadcasts. The impact went far beyond news and entertainment. By the end of the Thirties, around 11,000 elementary and secondary schools in mainland Britain had radio sets and tuned in to the BBC's excellent educational programmes.

'This is not the age of pamphleteers. It is the age of the engineer. The spark-plug is mightier than the sword.'

Lancelot Hogben, professor and author

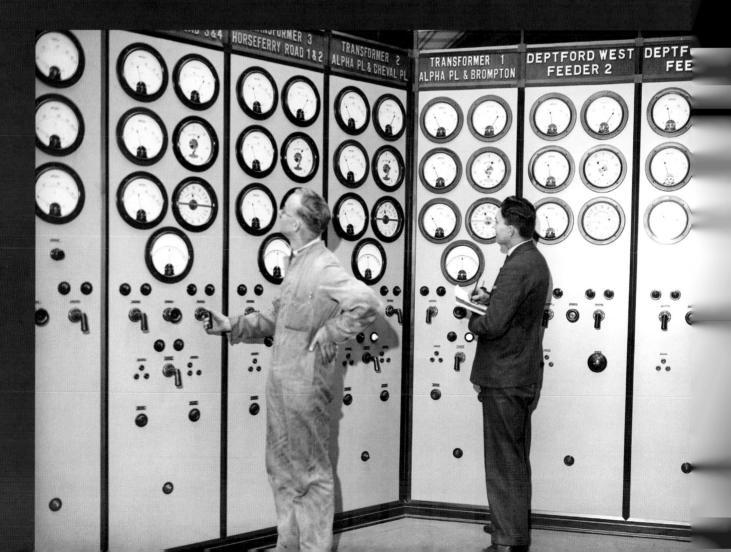

ELECTRIFYING THE NATION
Electricity was the key source of energy in the Thirties, and constructing the supply system was a massive project. Here (far left), a 51-ton stator – the stationary component of a generator – built in Birmingham is delivered for installation at a power station in Wembley in 1933. Battersea power station was built on the river right in the heart of London: these technicians (bottom left) are checking dials monitoring transformers and feeders in late 1932. The two lofty workmen (centre left) were at work on the insulators of the Central Electricity Board towers at Dagenham. By 1933, the National Grid of high-voltage transmission lines was almost complete, and Britain had one of the world's best electricity supply systems. Electricity had the effect of shifting industry from the North and Wales to the Midlands and Southeast. By 1938 the electricity industry was employing 325,000 – double the figure for 1924.

The number of electricity consumers shot up from just 730,000 in 1920 to 9 million by 1939. New customers were being added at the rate of 750,000 a year, and two in three houses were wired up. The first wave of electrical appliances in homes were vacuum cleaners, refrigerators, cookers and radios, but electricity was reaching into every part of life. It powered broadcasting, the cinema, trains, trams and trolley buses. It was used in the new dangerous-looking machines for permanent hair waves: this intrepid woman (near left), seen in 1934, seems on the point of being electrocuted rather than coiffured. The team of workers below are constructing an electrical clock at Paddington Station in 1935.

PRESS WARS

News abounded, and it was a wonderful time to be a reader of popular newspapers. Circulation battles reached such intensity it was said that a whole Welsh family could be clothed from head to foot for the price of eight weeks' reading of the *Daily Express*, which showered the Principality with free gifts. The *Daily Herald* began it by offering its readers a set of Dickens novels in 16 volumes for 11 shillings (55p in today's money, now worth at least £20), which it said was 'worth four guineas' (£4.20). The paper's owner, Lord Southwood, claimed that this was 'just a figure of speech' and that a profit could be made on 11 shillings.

The *Daily Express, Daily Mail* and *News Chronicle* hit back, offering their readers Dickens sets for 10 shillings (50p), selling more than 300,000 sets between them and losing £36,000 in the process. Canvassers were sent round the country lavishing cameras, tea-sets, cutlery, coats, shirts and trousers on those who signed up to become registered readers. After giving away thousands of pairs of silk stockings, the *Daily Express* returned to books, offering 12 volumes of classic novels for 10 shillings. Not to be outdone, the magazine *John Bull* retaliated with 12 volumes of classic novels for 8s 9d. The *Express* dropped its price to 7s 6d, and sold 115,000 sets for a loss of £12,000. The *Herald* turned to 'four guinea' encyclopaedias at 11 shillings – and were undercut by the *Express*.

It cost a proprietor real money to wage war. The *Daily Herald* (years later to be reborn as *The Sun*) spent £1,325,000 in boosting its circulation from 400,000

DAILY BREAD
Workmen dismantle the famous clock as part of the remodelling of the *Daily Telegraph* building in Fleet Street. The British press was a phenomenon. No other country got near its massive circulation figures. The two big quality dailies, *The Times* and the *Telegraph*, sold almost a million copies a day between them. The *News of the World* reached a circulation of 3.8 million in 1939 – and its great rival, *The People*, was snapping at its heels. Circulation wars took many forms – cheap editions of Dickens and Shakespeare, cash prizes, free pairs of socks. Here, the *Daily Express* is subsidising loaves of bread.

to 1,750,000, at a cost of about £1 a reader. Beaverbrook spent his money to greater effect. It cost him £123,000, or 8s 7d a reader, to bring in an additional 300,000 readers. When the circulation war finally came to an end, the *Daily Express* had a circulation of more than 2 million – the largest for a daily paper anywhere in the world.

Charles Dickens reappeared in a final *Mail* versus *Express* skirmish. The great Victorian novelist had left behind him a Life of Christ, written for his children. He had specified that it was not to be published until they had all gone. The death of Sir Henry Dickens, last of the children, released it for the *Daily Mail* to pay £40,000 for exclusive rights – about £1 a word. The *Express* waited for the first promotion posters to go up, with Dickens looking out from beneath a crown of thorns, then took the gloss off the *Mail*'s scoop with an article revealing for the first time that late in life Dickens had an affair with the actress Ellen Ternan.

'The Conciliator'

By far the most influential journalist of the day was Geoffrey Dawson, the editor of *The Times*. Dawson was ferociously bright, a fellow of All Souls College, Oxford, and a former civil servant in South Africa who mingled as easily with the Establishment as his newspaper did. It was his second stint in charge of the elite's

FROM HOT METAL TO HOT NEWS
Compositors set type on linotype machines for a national newspaper in London in 1930 (above). Compositing was a skilled and well-paid trade, and the powerful Fleet Street print unions ensured that the use of hot metal machines like this survived into the computer age 50 years later. Newspapers were able to endure the arcane 'Spanish practices' that the unions used to ensure high wages only because of their vast readerships. In the Thirties more than two thirds of all over-16s in Britain read a national daily, and four in five read a national Sunday paper. There was also a strong local and provincial press, with newspapers like the *Leeds Mercury* that this newspaper boy is selling on a street corner in West Yorkshire (right).

daily paper. He had been editor under Lord Northcliffe from 1912, but resigned in 1919, disillusioned with the way the proprietor used the paper to promote his own political interests. Dawson returned in 1923 after Northcliffe died and ownership passed to his fellow Old Etonian, the more amenable John Jacob Astor.

Dawson now began using *The Times* to further his own ideas, much as Northcliffe had. He was close to both Baldwin and Chamberlain and, after Hitler came to power in 1933, he actively endorsed their policies of appeasement towards the Nazi dictator. Dawson was an old friend and frequent dining companion of Edward Wood, who became a pro-appeasement foreign secretary as Lord Halifax. He was also a member of the so-called 'Cliveden set', the circle around Nancy Astor, which met at the Astor's country house, Cliveden in Buckinghamshire, and favoured friendly relations with Nazi Germany. He was a member of the Anglo-German Fellowship and ensured that *The Times* made little reference to German anti-semitism. 'The Thunderer', as the paper had once been called for its robust views, became 'The Conciliator'.

Dawson can take the credit for a famous and long-lasting innovation: in January 1930 *The Times* ran its first crossword puzzle. Within a few weeks, an editorial in the paper boasted of 'overwhelming evidence' that the best brains in the country – 'ministers of the crown, provosts of colleges, King's Counsels and the rest' – were finding the crossword 'just the thing to fill up odd moments'. One such was M R James, the provost of Eton and author of bestselling collections of ghost stories. James boiled his morning eggs for the time it took him to complete the crossword, the paper said, and he 'hates a hard-boiled egg'.

On 1 March, 1930, the paper published an all-Latin puzzle, confident that the men who ran Britain were comfortable with the classics. Readers who knew the answer to 'Horace calls Tarentum this' (Lacedaemonium) might, like Dawson, be a trifle self-satisfied and fixed in their ways. But they were most unlikely to abandon the nation's traditional values for the frenzy and mass murder that was infecting their opposite numbers in the elites of Soviet Russia and Germany.

Daily, weekly and monthly variety

The British were the most voracious newspaper readers on earth. Provincial newspapers were strong – 'God the Father, God the Son and God the *Yorkshire Post*', they said in 'God's own county' – but national newspapers were a phenomenon, selling 10.5 million copies a day. Most of that went to the popular papers, with eye-catching photographs and strip cartoons, but *The Times* and *Daily Telegraph* sold almost a million between them – the lion's share to the *Telegraph* – and minorities were also catered for. The communist *Daily Worker* was founded in 1930. The *Daily Herald* was backed by the TUC. The *News Chronicle*, the *Manchester Guardian* and the *New Statesman* magazine were generally sympathetic to the Left.

Picture Post, a topical news magazine of photographic essays, was launched in 1938. Within a year it had a circulation of 2 million. The most successful women's magazine, meanwhile, was *Women's Own*, which progressed so well from its launch in 1932 that it was joined five years later by *Woman*, a rival with a mix of romantic short stories, recipes, fashion, cosmetics and hints on running a home.

Almost all the papers printed horoscopes – only the *Daily Herald*, *Sunday Times* and *Observer* felt them to be beneath their dignity. The best-known astrologer was R H Naylor of the *Sunday Express*. He also wrote for a bestselling

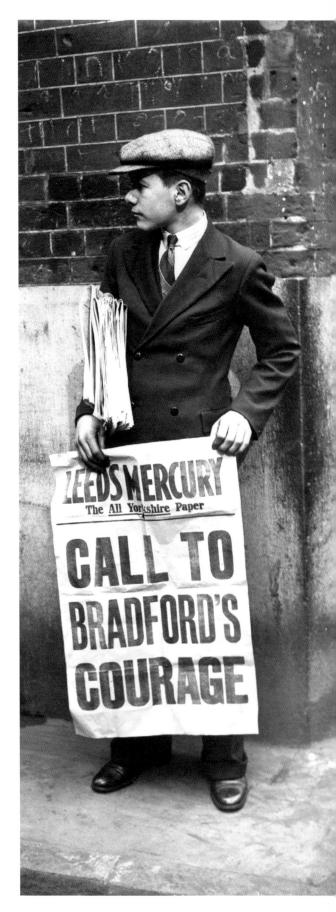

THE NEWS IN PICTURES

The *Picture Post* was launched in October 1938 as a topical news magazine of photographic essays. Within a year, it had a circulation of 2 million. The small but high quality Leica camera could capture people at their most unaware and natural. The photographer used it much as a traditional reporter used a notebook, to create a new type of 'candid camera' reportage. This had been brilliantly exploited by Stefan Lorant as editor of the *Münchner Illustrierte Presse*, before he was forced to flee Nazi Germany shortly after Hitler came to power. Instead of returning to his native Hungary, Lorant came to London to work as an editor and founded the monthly *Lilliput*, a copy of a successful German magazine, *Querschnitt*. Then, with publisher Edward Hulton, he launched the *Picture Post*.

Not surprisingly, given the year and Lorant's staunch opposition to Hitler, the drift to war was the dominant theme of the new publication. In February 1939, with Hitler devouring Czechoslovakia, the French General Berthomet was featured on the cover in Tuareg dress (right). At the end of May, with the crisis in Europe getting ever closer to home, the cover story was the way auxiliary firemen across Britain were preparing to combat the fires that would follow German bombing raids (below). There was still time – just – for some fun in August when bathing belles at Brighton held high a *Picture Post* balloon (far right).

WEEKLY ESCAPE
Comics were read avidly by children from all backgrounds. These two girls (left) are on a luxury Pullman train from London Victoria, a sure sign of money in the family, while the boy below is comfortably stretched out on the window ledge of his terraced house home. George Orwell wrote a famous essay on 'Boys' Weeklies' in 1939. Boys' comics, he observed, had two basic beliefs that 'nothing ever changes, and foreigners are funny'. Many boys' comics found eager readers among girls, too. Comics aimed specifically at girls, like *Crystal*, offered escape. 'What child bound all day by an elementary school classroom or the walls of a factory,' Orwell commented, 'does not long to be cruising, skating, riding or giving a garden party in an Emir's palace?'

sixpenny monthly, *Prediction*, which covered the ground from palmistry and clairvoyance to spiritualism and hypnotism. *Old Moore's* had been the most famous almanac since correctly predicting a snowfall on Derby Day in Victorian times. But the title had never been copyrighted and the troubled times gave such a boost to the sooth-saying industry that nine Old Moore's – each with different and often clashing predictions – were being published every Christmas.

Children's comics were another growth area. The old much-loved staples, *Gem* and *Magnet*, had, George Orwell thought, two basic beliefs: 'nothing ever changes, and foreigners are funny'. The French were always Froggies and had pointed beards, the Italians were Dagoes and played barrel-organs, the Chinese had saucer-shaped hats and pigtails. They usually carried a single story, written by the same person. It is not surprising, then, that a raft of new comics – *Wizard, Rover, Skipper, Hotspur, Champion, Modern Boy* – now appeared. Each issue had seven or eight different serials, so they gave their readers much greater variety.

School stories aside, the favourite subjects of these new comics were the Wild West, the Frozen North, the Foreign Legion, the Great War (Air Force or Secret Service, never the trenches), Tarzan-type jungle stories, football, Robin Hood, Cavaliers and Roundheads, and scientific invention. Orwell found that 'Death-rays, Martians, invisible men, robots, helicopters and interplanetary rockets figure largely'. He credited H G Wells with being the father of this 'scientifiction': his classic, *The Time Machine*, had been popular since 1895. Wells was still writing, but *The Shape of Things to Come*, which he published in 1933, was not a piece of futuristic sci-fi but a warning against the evils of Fascism.

Girls had comics, too. *Crystal* featured The Fourth Formers at St Chads School. *Silver Star* offered romantic serials such as 'Love's Sinner' for older readers.

Vicar unfrocked

The most read-about churchman of the Thirties, to the chagrin of the Anglican Church, was the rector of the little village of Stiffkey in Norfolk. At Norwich Cathedral on 21 October, 1932 – Trafalgar Day, as it happened, which celebrated Horatio Nelson, a man born in a vicarage not far from Stiffkey – the bishop of Norwich, with the dean and canons, proceeded in solemn state to the Beauchamp chapel. They had come to pass judgment on Rev Harold Davidson, who scurried in after them, a little late, clutching a silk top hat and accompanied by his sister.

Davidson had arrived in Stiffkey aged 31 in 1906. He conducted services every Sunday, then on Monday left his wife and five children in the rectory and caught the train from Wells-next-the-Sea to London. There he spent the rest of the week badgering young girls with faintly lewd suggestions. Some of them were prostitutes, others were waitresses in ABC tea shops and Lyons Corner Houses. Some were amused by the old man. Some were not. The bishop proceeded to deprive him of holy orders for conduct unbecoming: he was degraded and 'defrocked'. Davidson left the cathedral, shouting angrily, as a layman.

Now penniless and abandoned, Davidson took to amusing the public to keep body and soul together. One of his stunts was to threaten to starve himself to death in a barrel on the sands at Blackpool. The police arrested him on a charge of attempted suicide. He was acquitted and won an action for damages against Blackpool Corporation, in which he was awarded £382. His notoriety was such that he could pull in large crowds by appearing with a dead whale at a Bank Holiday fair on Hampstead Heath. A circus hired him to appear with lions in a cage. This, alas, was his undoing. He and the lions were a threepenny sideshow at Skegness in July 1937 when a lion began to maul him. The trainer, aptly enough a 16-year-old girl, Irene Violet Sumner, made valiant efforts to rescue him. In vain.

MISGUIDED VICAR

The Rector of Stiffkey, Harold Davidson, with his daughter Patricia after a court hearing at Church House, Westminster, on 30 March, 1932. The case followed scandalous allegations that his work with prostitutes in London was not the sort of behaviour expected of a man of the cloth. His case gave the newspapers much to moralise about. He was defrocked later that year and eventually came to a much stickier end, attacked by a lion in Skegness.

Monster of the deep

The great diversionary story was the Loch Ness Monster. In 1933 an AA patrolman claimed to have seen a serpent-like shape in the waters of the loch. Other claims rolled in, from residents and tourists alike. Most of the Catholic monks of Fort Augustus on the lochside said they had seen the monster, and the Father Superior agreed that he had been aware of it for some years.

A big game hunter went to investigate and found a strange spoor in the shingle by the loch. The Natural History Museum said that the spoor resembled that of a hippopotamus. The scientist Sir Arthur Keith said that the monster might be a reptile with legs, but he suspected it was an illusion and that a psychologist would be more useful than a zoologist.

'Nessie', as the monster was affectionately called, did marvels for the Scottish tourist trade. Theories abounded. A local ghillie said it was an old blind salmon. A visitor said they had seen it crossing a road with a sheep in its mouth. An old woman disappeared – when her body was found on the moors, it was said that she had been carried there by the monster. The Royal Scottish Museum thought it might be a large tuna or shark that had come into the loch from the sea. A popular theory was that it was a whale that had entered the loch when it was small, and was now too big to get back to sea. A popular film was made, *The Secret of the Loch*, which showed only the odd glimpse of underwater shapes, but enough people saw it for the profits to endow a bed for divers at Greenwich Hospital.

News of Nessie spread. A Japanese paper described the monster wandering the heaths where Macbeth had met the three weird sisters. The *Berliner Illustrierte* said the monster had been caught and was on exhibition in Edinburgh. It ran pictures of it taken by the 'famous Scottish zoologist, Professor MacKeenkool'. The issue was dated 1 April, showing that some Germans still had a sense of humour. As the decade continued, though, such laughs would be at a premium.

BIRTH OF A LEGEND
This picture of Nessie, the Loch Ness Monster, was first published on 19 April, 1934, following widespread reporting of a sighting the previous year. It was one of two images known as the 'surgeon's photographs', supposedly taken by Colonel Robert Kenneth Wilson. It was later revealed to have been a hoax by Christian Spurling, who claimed on his deathbed that he had helped big-game hunter Marmaduke Wetherell to stage the picture, also aided by Wetherell's son, Ian. But by then the story of Nessie had a life of its own. The group of monks angling on Loch Ness below are from the nearby Fort Augustus Abbey, where most of the resident order claimed to have seen the monster. It was said that references to a monster in the loch went back all the way to St Columba in AD 565, when the saint was said to have prevented the monster from eating a Pict.

UNEQUAL FORTUNES

From 1931 to 1935 the number of people officially classed as unemployed in Britain never dropped below 2 million. In the bleak winter of 1932–3, the total climbed to almost 3 million. In other words, a quarter of the working population was out of work. One in four passed their days in enforced idleness, on a street corner, in a library reading room. These official statistics excluded farm labourers, the self-employed, married women and others, which meant that the true unemployment figure was even higher.

A PLEA FOR WORK A man makes his own protest against unemployment with a home-made sandwich board in 1935.

THREE ENGLANDS

Seasonal unemployment could swell the ranks of the jobless. Farms required more hands at harvest than at other times of the year. Building labourers were laid off in the winter, as were waiters and fairground staff in summer resorts such as Blackpool and Brighton. Even in the otherwise healthy car industry, winter was a slack time, for cars sold best in spring and summer.

Since the slump was global, the effects of it were, too. Countries such as Argentina, Canada, South Africa and Australia had all lost customers for their food and wool, and as a consequence had less capital with which to buy manufactured goods from Britain. By 1929, British exports had crept back up to just over three-quarters of their pre-war level, but two years later, in 1931, they had plummeted back to half their 1913 level.

Two towns

A word of caution is needed here. As Dickens wrote in *A Tale of Two Cities*, his novel set in London and Paris at the time of the French Revolution, 'It was the best of times. It was the worst of times.' His words could equally have applied to the state of Britain in the 1930s.

Choose two cities or towns. Let Dagenham in Essex be one, the prosperous one. London County Council was building its largest new housing estate there. It had 18,000 houses in 1930. The Londoners who were rehoused there found gardens, bathrooms, kitchens and electric light waiting for them in homes that were palaces compared to the slums they had left in the East End. Ford built a brand new factory nearby on a green field site. The whole place purred with prosperity. Ford was doubling its workforce every three years.

Now consider Jarrow, on the south side of the Tyne in what was then County Durham (now Tyne and Wear). Jarrow had industrial pedigree when Dagenham was still green fields. Palmer's shipyard pioneered rolled armour plate there in 1856. It built hundreds of proud warships, colliers and cargo vessels. Palmers was the town's lifeblood, employing three men in four. In 1930, the yard was reeling. By 1933, it was finished. The only great ship that came to Jarrow was the *Olympic*, sister ship of the *Titanic*, and she came to be dismantled for scrap. Ellen Wilkinson, Jarrow's Labour MP, wrote a famous book called *The Town That was Murdered*. Where Dagenham was teeming with new life, Jarrow was dying.

A traveller's view

When the writer J B Priestley journeyed across England in 1933, he found that there were 'three Englands'. The first was Old England, the country of cathedrals,

COUNTRY MEETS TOWN
In a photograph from 1934 that seems to epitomise two of Priestley's 'three Englands', harvesters gather their crops almost under the shadow of the great Cunard White Star liner *Queen Mary*, being built over the water at John Brown's shipyard on Clydebank. Britain's agriculture and shipbuilding were hard-pressed by the economic conditions of the decade, leaving many workers unemployed. Both would be rescued only by the coming of war, which created unprecedented demand for ships and homegrown produce.

FARMING INCOMES IN FREEFALL

A Conservative poster in the 1931 election (left) urged people to vote for the new National Government in order to protect British growers. Ever since the repeal of the Corn Laws, it had been held that cheap food imports were more beneficial to the economy than shoring up local produce with expensive subsidies. The long Depression followed by the onset of war at the end of the Thirties finally brought a change of heart.

Arable farming was in serious decline, with more than 3 million acres passing out of cultivation in the years between the wars. Many farms switched to rearing livestock, like this man (bottom left) with two of his lambs at Blindley Heath in Surrey. A further 60,000 acres a year was being taken from agriculture by road and house building. There was a great outcry against the suburban sprawl – of London, in particular, which was partly controlled by Act of Parliament in 1935. The landed gentry, also long in decline, faced fresh catastrophes from the fall in farm incomes. *The Times* claimed that half of Norfolk was owned not by the landowners but by the banks. A government report described choked ditches, overgrown hedges and dilapidated fences and gates. 'The landscape of 1938', it concluded, 'had in many places become neglected and unkempt.'

One bright spot on the agricultural horizon was the growth in market gardening, largely for the burgeoning canning industry. Before the First World War, most tinned fruit and vegetables came from America. By the end of the Thirties, citrus fruits and peaches apart, the bulk of the business went to British growers. Peas became the most important vegetable crop, and raspberries, strawberries and plums the main fruits. Smallholders, many owned by ex-servicemen, dominated market gardening, but it demanded long, hard hours of work to make it pay. Another potentially profitable crop was flowers. Here (right), early spring daffodils are being picked in Cornwall for the London market in 1934.

manors and inns, parsons and squires, the place that foreign tourists visited, that appeared on chocolate boxes and Christmas cards. It was as alien to the real England, Priestley said, as a horse and trap was to the motor-racing circuit at Brooklands. The country had moved on.

As the decade began, another traveller, H V Morton, wrote of the 'economic and social cancer' that lay behind the beauty of the countryside. Everywhere, he said, the story was the same: cornland going back to grass, estates breaking up when the owners died, farmers crippled by mortgages, even keeping cattle was a folly when 'the Roast Beef of Old England comes so cheaply from the Argentine'.

The price of corn fell to 20s 9d (not quite 90p) a quarter, the lowest it had been since the Civil War nearly 300 years before. In East Anglia, farmers were losing at least £5 on every acre of wheat, 5 shillings on every sheep. Land was worth a quarter of what it had been before the Depression. Fields were abandoned

FARMERS' PROTEST
Marchers wearing banners and carrying a sheaf of wheat set out from Tower Hill in London on a Farmers' March to Westminster in February 1939. Farmers were hard hit by the sharp fall in agricultural prices after 1929. Some mechanised farms in East Anglia and Hampshire were able to compete with cheap cereal imports from Canada and Australia, but most of Britain's farms could not, and labour drifted away from the land. These demonstrators could not know it, but the coming war would revitalise the farming market: farmers would soon be selling every ear of wheat and every sack of potatoes that they could grow. From having a glut of deteriorating and unprofitable farmland – some of it left untilled for rough shooting – the country would move within two years to putting even the most marginal land under the plough.

to brambles and weeds. Farmers demonstrated with banners that read: 'Wanted in 1914. Abandoned in 1930.' Such protests had no effect. The cities wanted cheap food and that meant Canadian wheat and frozen New Zealand lamb.

In some great houses on once profitable estates, the families retreated from wing to wing, the roofs and casements rotting behind them. A third of the great houses of Shropshire disappeared. The owners of sporting estates were hard hit by the cumulative effects of the Wall Street Crash. The American sportsmen who had paid top dollar to shoot in Britain had disappeared. By 1932, the makers of sporting guns faced ruin. Arable farming was the hardest hit. More than 3 million acres passed out of cultivation between the wars. Market gardening fared better, expanding with demand from canners for fruit and vegetables.

In this climate weekenders began to snap up country cottages as people left the land. Farm workers in East Anglia earned as little as 30 shillings a week. Their diet hardly differed from that of the poor in industrial cities. A supper of white bread and margarine, tinned sardines and tea was the main meal, with bread and cheese and pickles at midday.

Industrial England

The second England identified on Priestley's journey was 19th century England. This was the industrial nation of coal, steel, cotton, wool and railways. It took up much of the Midlands and the North, but could be found elsewhere, with row upon row of back-to-back houses, square-faced chapels, mill chimneys, slag heaps and tips, pubs, railway yards, slums and fried fish shops. For the better-off there were detached villas with monkey-puzzle trees, grill rooms, good-class drapers, and Unionist and Liberal clubs. The tough and enterprising, once they had made a tidy fortune, slipped out of this 'mucky England of their making', and settled amid the charms of Old England, where their children, 'well schooled, groomed and finished', were little different from the old land-owning families.

In Leeds, there were 33,000 back-to-back houses, built 70 to 80 to the acre, with small and squalid rooms. Industry had turned the once green and pleasant land into a 'wilderness of dirty bricks', with blackened fields and poisoned rivers. Priestley found this in Wolverhampton, St Helens, Bolton, Gateshead, Jarrow, Shotton … It was as if the country had 'devoted a hundred years of its life to keeping gigantic sooty pigs'. He thought that Hebburn on Tyneside looked as much like an ordinary town as 'a dustbin looks like a drawing-room'. Its shipyards were silent and rotting, its skilled men hanging about the streets as if 'waiting for Doomsday'. Each day, men who had built fine ships went out in a down-at-heel old ship's boat to catch a few fish to give to the families of the unemployed. The town's spirit was not yet broken – it had an orchestra, a ladies' and a children's choir, gym classes, a camping and rambling club – but Priestley felt its self-respect was draining away. This was a working town and it had no work.

> ## The less lucky in industrial England 'were very unlucky indeed … [with] monstrously long hours of work, miserable wages, and surroundings in which they lived like black beetles at the back of a disused kitchen stove.'
>
> J B Priestley in *English Journey*, published in 1934

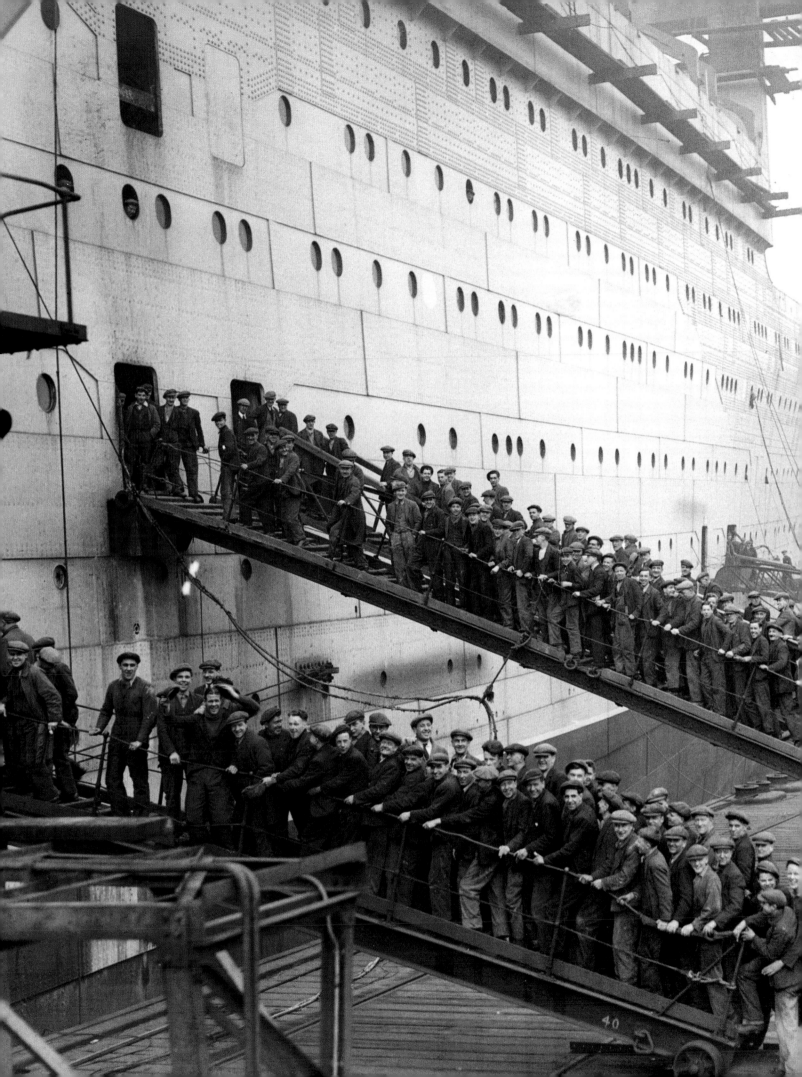

THE LUCKY ONES

Some of the hundreds of men employed to build the *Queen Mary* return to complete their shift after the dinner break. At this stage – March 1935 – the ship was still known in John Brown's shipyard as 'Liner 534'. A huge range of skills was needed to build a great ocean liner, the biggest, most sophisticated, luxurious and arguably most beautiful mode of transport ever created. She needed joiners, precision engineers, plumbers, welders, glaziers, electricians, boilermakers and above all riveters. Every piece of the ship's hull was held together by rivets, literally millions of which would be hammered home in the construction of a liner. The smiling rivet boy below is Patrick Breslin. He worked on the *Queen Elizabeth*, which was commissioned from John Brown's yard in 1936, the year the *Queen Mary* made her maiden voyage.

The 'third England'

Priestley thought the true birthplace of what he identified as the third England was America. It was a brand new place of arterial roads and by-passes, petrol stations, giant cinemas and dance halls, cocktail bars, Woolworths, 'factory girls looking like actresses', greyhound tracks and swimming pools. Coming into London from the north, he passed miles of semi-detached houses, all with their little garages and wireless sets, where people read magazines about film stars, and had things like swimming costumes and tennis rackets that were quite unknown in the terraces of industrial England.

This new world was materialistic. People needed money to live there, but not that much. Its clean factories – all glass, white tiles and chromium plate, a far cry from the grimy brick-built mills and factories of the North – mass produced cheap luxuries and new electrical goods such as vacuum cleaners, electric toasters and gramophones. It was, Priestley thought, a democratic place: '… in this England, for the first time in history, Jack and Jill are nearly as good as their master and mistress.' It was cleaner, tidier and healthier than industrial Britain, but Priestley, who hailed from Bradford, could not help thinking it had fewer 'solid lumps of character'.

SMALL BUSINESS – SERVING THE CUSTOMER WITH ESSENTIALS
The delivery boy pedalling furiously on his bicycle to make home deliveries was part of the familiar street scene in the Thirties. Mr Pierce the fishmonger (above left) had a specially converted bicycle to take his fresh fish to customers as he toured the streets of Margate in 1935. The tray is built in a V-shape to hold a good stock of ice. This London milk vendor (left) was doing the rounds with his cart in 1937. He prided himself on bottling and delivering his milk on the same day that it came up from the dairy farm. Cockles and mussels, winkles, eels and shrimps, were sold from stalls in all the big cities, as well as being treats for day-trippers on outings to the seaside. They got there through people like this cheerful cockle gatherer (right), photographed in 1936 at low tide on the beach at Penclawdd in South Wales, accompanied by a boy and donkey.

Regional differences

The figures backed Priestley up. The situation was worst in heavy industry and the mines; pottery workers and seamen were also hit hard. The old Victorian backbone of the country was almost broken, and shipbuilding had fared the worst. By 1932, almost 60 per cent of shipyard workers were without a job. The great Cammell Laird yard in Birkenhead had just a single dredger on its order book. Iron and steel and the mines were in dire straits, too, at 48.5 per cent and 41.2 per cent of workers unemployed. Cotton was slightly better, at 31 per cent. The average unemployment across all industries was 22.9 per cent, but since this figure included the grim totals for the old industries, the real contrast was much greater. Some towns, like St Albans and Oxford, barely felt the slump at all.

The pain was regional, sometimes microscopically so. In South Wales, for example, three-quarters of the men in Brynmawr and Dowlais and two thirds of men in Merthyr had no work in 1934. In contrast, the coastal towns were little affected. The anthracite and tinplate areas in the west Wales coalfields, and the

Neath and Swansea valleys, also suffered much less than the eastern half. Between them, the Merthyr, Rhondda and Aberdare valleys had half the unemployed of South Wales. In an attempt to address the situation, in 1934 the government created 'special areas' for state aid. These embraced South Wales, Tyneside, West Cumberland and industrial Scotland. Northern Ireland was badly hit, too, its shipyards and linen mills idle, but it lay beyond the scope of Westminster legislation. Together, these areas had two-thirds of all Britain's unemployed.

It was difficult for the depressed areas to recover. Unemployment was not only much higher there, but it lasted much longer. The new industries, powered by electricity, located themselves close to the big consumer markets in the Southeast and the Midlands, with the result that only a small fraction of the jobless in the Southeast were out of work for more than a year, compared to more than a third in Wales. The jobless rate in London and the Southeast never went much above 6 per cent and the Midlands, too, were relatively unscathed. Wales and Northern Ireland were four times worse off. It was only occasionally that a run-down region found itself well-placed for a growth industry. ICI brought chemical plants and much needed employment to Teesside near the decaying Durham pit villages and the silent shipyards of the Wear.

BEANS MEANS ... WORK
Women canning green beans on a production line at Wisbech in Cambridgeshire in 1934. The Thirties saw a big increase in the amount of produce grown and canned in Britain. The work was still labour intensive, but production line techniques were honed throughout the decade. The increase in productivity would be a vital factor in the coming war.

BASKET WORKERS
Jobs were found whenever possible for ex-
servicemen crippled in mind or body during the
Great War. These men at the Cardiff Institute in
1938 are making huge baskets – resembling
Welsh coracles in size and construction – to be
used for loading oil cake in South Africa

BLEAK BRITAIN

Idleness made the mills and industrial towns appear darker and more satanic than ever. For mile upon mile, the landscape was slag-heaps, scrap metal, rotting wharves, weed-infested shunting yards and gaunt men sifting through coal tips or fishing by the banks of a scum-cold canal. The writer George Orwell felt that it was a 'kind of duty' for the better-off to see and smell the labyrinthine slums.

Orwell caught an essence of the depression from a train window. At the back of one slum terraced house, he saw a young woman kneeling on stones, trying to unblock a drainpipe with a stick. He saw her clearly, 'her sacking apron, her clumsy clogs, her arms reddened by the cold'. Her face was round and pale, the exhausted face of the slum girl worn out by need and toil, with the most desolate expression he had ever seen. What he saw was not the ignorant suffering of an animal. 'She knew well enough what was happening to her', he wrote, 'understood as well as I did how dreadful a destiny it was to be kneeling there in the bitter cold, on the slimy stones of a slum backyard, poking a stick up a foul drainpipe.'

Voluntary help

Charities and volunteers were a tremendous force in offsetting poverty. The Rotary clubs, the Inner Wheel, the Women's Institutes had thousands of members doing their bit to help. Volunteers manned soup kitchens, packed Christmas parcels for needy families, or helped to pay for recreation halls and allotments. Towns Women's Guilds helped the blind, orphans, unmarried mothers, prisoners, aged governesses, shipwrecked sailors and many more. Family planning clinics and a quarter of maternity and child welfare centres were kept going by voluntary effort. There were 1,013 voluntary hospitals in 1935, providing a third of the country's hospital beds, kept afloat by flag days, appeals, bazaars and donations.

Individual benefactors were important. The Carnegie UK Trust, founded in 1913 by the Scots-born American industrialist, continued to fund everything from public libraries to village halls and music festivals. An Indian steel magnate set up the Ratan Tata foundation for social work. Edward Harkness, an American whose family made a fortune in Standard Oil, was another man of great generosity. He provided £2 million in 1930 for the Pilgrim Trust and to endow scholarships, 'prompted by his admiration for what Great Britain had done in the 1914–18 war, and by his ties of affection for the land from which he drew his descent'. The most spectacular philanthropist of all was a home-grown tycoon. Lord Nuffield had started work as William Morris in a bicycle shop at 16. By 1940 he had given more than £10 million to charity. His money came from his car plants, the biggest at Cowley in Oxford. He gave £4 million to the university, £2 million to medical research, and £1 million to found a new post-graduate college of social sciences.

Orwell's insight

The poor lived on white bread and margarine, cans of corned beef or sardines, potatoes and sugared tea. They had no fresh fruit, no nourishing wholemeal bread. The result, Orwell said, was the 'physical degeneracy' on view in the industrial towns. The people of Sheffield, for example, were physically so small they seemed to be 'a population of troglodytes'. Very few had their own teeth: anyone over 30 who did was considered an abnormality. In Wigan, Orwell stayed in a house with five people, the oldest was 42, the youngest a boy of 15. The boy was the only one who possessed a single tooth of his own. 'Teeth is just misery', a woman said. It was best to 'get shut of them' as early in life as possible.

Orwell described a house in the Scholes quarter of Wigan that cost 9s 6d a week to rent. It was a two up, two down, with a coal hole. The walls were falling to pieces, water came through the roof, the floor was lopsided and the windows did not open. In another, smaller house – a one up, two down – with a leaking roof he found a family of ten, eight of them children: the corporation recognised they were overcrowded, but could not find a more suitable house for them. None of these houses had baths or lavatories. These were streets of back-to-backs, with two houses built as one, so that each side had a front door. The front houses faced onto the street, the back houses onto a yard with the lavatories and dustbins. Those living on the front might have a walk of 50 yards or more to the lavatory. In mining districts, subsidence from underground workings sometimes canted whole streets at an angle – jammed windows were commonplace.

Legend had it that the worst landlord was 'a fat wicked man, preferably a bishop', who lived high on the hog off his extortionate rents. The reality, Orwell found, was that it was the poor landlord – perhaps a widow who had invested all her money in three back-to-backs, inhabiting one of them and living off the rents of the others. She would never have the money for repairs. So roofs leaked, bugs thrived and as the houses became more decrepit they became more and more crowded, with the desperately poor spreading the rent among them.

Wigan – for all George Orwell and the music-hall jokes about 'Wigan Pier' – was by no means the worst. H V Morton was rather charmed by it. He liked its Italian gardens and the lake in its park, and the way the corporation insisted that buildings on the main streets were in Tudor style. He thought it was 'a spa' compared to Wednesbury and the Staffordshire pottery towns.

The hated Means Test

The drop in income for families when a job was lost was brutal. In Stockton-on-Tees, for example, families with a wage earner averaged £2 11s 6d a week, compared to those on the dole who had just £1. A study for the Ministry of Labour in 1937 reflected this, with falls of between two thirds and 45 per cent. During the row over the means test, dieticians worked out the minimum sum that a human being needed to stay alive. They estimated it at 5s 9d a week.

The dole, as unemployment benefit was called, was only paid as a right for 26 weeks. After that, claimants were subject to the despised Means Test. This was done by the local Public Assistance Committee (PAC) that had replaced the Poor Law Guardians. The maximum payment for a man was 15s 3d a week. This was only paid if the PAC was satisfied that the claimant had no other income – no savings, no relatives helping out and no part-time work. The process was humiliating for respectable, hard-working men, many of them skilled, who felt

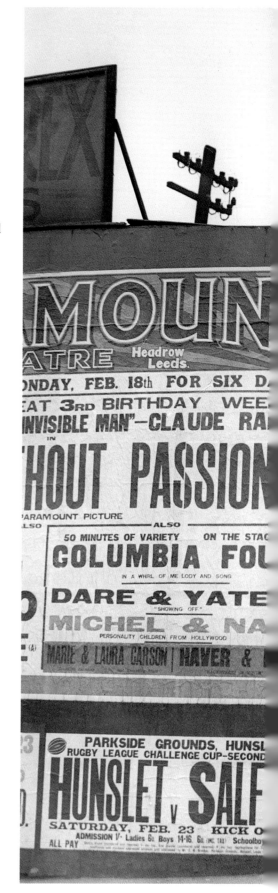

SCRAP FOR SALE
Potential customers rout about in a scrapyard in Leeds in 1935, on the lookout for cheap spare parts. There was plenty of demand. The car industry was one of the great successes of the decade. By 1939, Britain had 2 million privately owned cars, a 20-fold increase since 1919. The cost of a small car like an Austin Seven was just half what it had been in the Twenties.

themselves treated no better than vagrants under the old Poor Law. The 'relieving officers' who assessed a man's means visited his home, nosed into his life, looked at his furniture – and sometimes suggested he sell some of it. The dole money was cut if he had savings, or money from sons and daughters, or if he had a pensioner living in the household. It was an offence to keep any resources concealed. Many were found ineligible for benefit, others had it reduced. In Lancashire, for example, it was claimed that only 16 per cent were awarded full benefits, and that a third were debarred outright. Over the country as a whole, half of applicants got less than the maximum. There were cases where children and grandparents had to leave the family home because their earnings and pensions would have led to the head of the family having his dole money stopped.

The savings for the government in the first year were £24 million, but the cost in humiliation and family hardship was high. An unemployed Birmingham man killed himself after his benefit was cut to 10s 9d a week, with the threat of it being cut totally. The coroner declared it 'very distressing' and found that the Means Test had been the final straw in rendering him 'temporarily insane'.

Men cycled miles to look for work, or hung around factory gates, hoping for a few hours of casual work. In the mining districts, they went coal-picking, sifting through the slag heaps for scraps of coal. In Wigan, George Orwell saw men with

UNEMPLOYED IN THE THIRTIES
A man looks out over an industrial landscape as blighted and forlorn as the lives of the unemployed (right). The wreckage left behind by the decay of old industries, the heaps of cinders, the crumbling bricks and broken windows of abandoned factories, was like the detritus of a great war. The unemployed flocked to libraries to scan the jobs columns in the papers, but also simply to pass the time by reading (above). More books were issued by public libraries in the Thirties than ever before. About 100 million book loans were made in 1930 and nine years later the figure had climbed to 247 million. As well as public libraries, there were 'twopenny libraries' in stores like Boots. Book Clubs were founded throughout the decade, catering for the politically left, right and centre. And Allen Lane published the first sixpenny Penguin paperback in 1935.

'Unemployment is not an active state. Its keynote is boredom – a continuous sense of boredom.'

from a report on unemployment published in the 1930s

LIFE ON THE DOLE

The average unemployed family had an income of about 30 shillings a week. A change in diet accompanied the loss of a job: meat, eggs, fresh vegetables, butter and milk usually disappeared, to be replaced by margarine, condensed milk, bread and potatoes. George Orwell was shown the weekly budget of an unemployed miner and his wife. They had two children, one aged two years, the other 10 months. Here is how they spent their 32 shillings a week dole money:

Rent	9s ½d
Clothing Club	3s
Coal	2s
Gas	1s 3d
Milk	0s 10½d
Union fees	0s 3d
Insurance	0s 2d
Meat	2s 6d
Flour	3s 4d
Yeast	0s 4d
Potatoes	1s
Dripping	0s 10d
Margarine	0s 10d
Bacon	1s 2d
Sugar	1s 9d
Tea	1s
Jam	0s 7½d
Peas, cabbage	0s 6d
Carrots, onions	0s 4d
Quaker oats	0s 4½d
Soap, powders	0s 10d
TOTAL	£1 12s 0d

In addition, the family got three packets of dried milk a week for the baby from the Infants' Welfare Clinic. Orwell noted that the list left out many items: pepper, salt, vinegar, matches, razor blades, wear and tear on furniture and bedding, and so on. It included no 'luxuries', like beer or tobacco. If the man of the house smoked or drank, there would have to be a reduction in some of the staples in the list. Clothing Clubs, into which this miner was paying 3 shillings a week, were run by big drapers in all the big industrial towns. It was only through them that the unemployed were able to buy new clothes.

sacks and baskets scrabbling on slag-heaps that gave off sulphurous smoke from fires smouldering beneath the surface. He watched as some 200 ragged men, each with a sack and a coal-hammer, waited for a train carrying fresh slag from the mines. With the train doing almost 20mph, they hurled themselves aboard. It was dangerous: one man had lost both legs under a train a few weeks before Orwell's visit. At the slag-heap they shovelled the dirt out, while wives and children below picked out lumps of coal, the size of eggs or smaller. Then they trudged the two miles back to Wigan, with perhaps ninepence worth of coal in their sacks. And though it was waste coal, it was still theft to take it. Now and again, a colliery company prosecuted a man for coal-picking. The local magistrates would fine him 10 shillings, and his fellow coal-pickers would raise the money among themselves.

The struggle to survive bred fatalism, depression and apathy, but little violence and no revolution. The National Unemployed Workers Movement (NUWM) was the most militant. But it was closely allied to the communist party and official Labour leaders distrusted it, the more so after NUWM marchers clashed with police in Bristol in 1931 on their way to lobby the TUC conference. NUWM membership peaked at a claimed 100,000, and there were further clashes with police in Belfast, Birkenhead, Manchester and London in autumn 1932 as it campaigned against the means test. The fighting went on for three days in Birkenhead, with bottles and park railings used as missiles. Police charged at a demonstration in Parliament Square in Westminster.

A million people were said to have signed a petition to scrap the Means Test. It was carried by 2,500 marchers to London, who were greeted by crowds of workers in Hyde Park. The police charged with batons, and a hundred people were injured in violent scuffles. Most newspapers used the presence of the NUWM

THE HARDEST LIFE OF ALL

Miners suffered worst from unemployment, particularly in Wales, where these miners were photographed outside their cottages in Ebbw Vale on a bleak December day in 1934. That year, half the miners in the Methyr valley and 45 per cent in the Rhondda were out of work. The life they yearned to return to was brutal, but at least their families were better off than when there was no work. In 1930 these two miners (top right) stripped down to their underwear to cope with the intense heat underground at Tilmanstone Colliery in the Kent coalfield. The photograph was made possible by the recently developed 'Sashalite', a safe flash light which replaced earlier dangerous flash illumination in photography. Boys could start down the pit as young as 14 years. These pit boys (bottom right) are learning how to handle and harness a pit pony at Manvers Main Colliery at Mexborough in 1935. Training was vital, for the mines were death-traps. Over the five years to the end of 1931, more than 5,000 men and boys died in the mining industry, while 800,000 were injured.

to brand the marchers as Reds, claiming they had used the 'Bolshie' or Bolshevik tactic of baiting the police. The petititon was never delivered to Parliament. It seemed that it had been left in a London Underground cloakroom for safekeeping, and the cloakroom had lost it. Cynics observed that this avoided a re-run of the Chartist petition of 1848, where two-thirds of the signatures were found to be forgeries. A fresh burst of trouble in 1935 in South Wales and Sheffield accompanied the creation of the unpopular Unemployment Assistance Board, which superseded the PAC in dealing with the long-term unemployed.

The NUWM's influence, though, was already waning. The most common attitude among Durham miners, a report found to some surprise, was the determination to 'make the best of things'. There was little sense of grievance. Only a tiny proportion of the young unemployed in South Wales was politically motivated. It was wrong, another study said, to assume that their want and discontent was expressed in revolutionary attitudes.

The Jarrow March

The 'Jarrow crusade' was one of the few hunger marches not run by the NUWM. It was deliberately non-political, and its appeal to the public was all the more powerful for it. It was also one of the smallest marches. Just 200 Jarrow men walked to London with a petition. Local Conservative as well as Labour officials helped to organise it, and it was made clear that their crusade had nothing to do with a much larger march organised by the NUWM at the same time. Newspapers and news-reels felt it safe to give full and sympathetic coverage to such a non-Red march. The marchers were greeted with great goodwill in towns and villages along

LIFE IN THE MINES

Even in work, miners earned little enough. They were paid an average of around 10 shillings a shift, which should have brought in £3 a week, or around £150 a year. But there were always days when they were laid off, or struck a run of rock in a coal seam, or when machinery broke down. Any of these meant a loss of earnings. There were also regular wage stoppages of almost 5 shillings a week – for union fees, the miners' benevolent fund, unemployment and health insurance, plus a shilling a week to the colliery for the hire of lamps and sharpening tools. Then there were the 'Death Stoppages'. When a miner was killed at work, his fellows in the pit made a subscription, usually of a shilling each, for his widow. It was collected by the colliery company and deducted from their pay. As a result, the average gross earnings of British miners in 1934 was £115 11s 6d for the year. There were big differences between regions. Scottish miners were the best off with £133 2s 8d, Durham miners the worst with £105. They needed their famous annual gala to keep their spirits up.

Death Stoppages were all too commonplace. Every year, one miner in 900 was killed, and one in six injured. Over a working life of 40 years or so, a miner was unlikely to avoid injury and the odds of being killed were about 20 to 1. No other job was as dangerous as this, except perhaps fishing: one sailor in 1,300 was killed every year, but as there were fewer fishermen the proportion was higher. The dangers in a pit were manifest. Gas explosions could be set off by the spark from a pick axe striking stone, by defective lamps, or by 'gob fires', which smouldered spontaneously in coal dust. Explosions accounted for the worst disasters, but there was also constant attrition from roof falls. Many miners preferred the old wooden pit props to the newer metal ones, because they could hear them creaking before they gave way. One innovation of the 1930s that did get general approval among miners was the introduction of pit-head baths. Rather than trudging home dirty to scrub off the coal dust in a tin bath, these men are about to use the pit-head baths at Ellington Colliery, Northumberland, in 1936. Instead of lockers, their clothes are strung up to the ceiling on ropes.

the way and in London at the end, but although it has become the lasting symbol of the Depression in Britain, it achieved very little for Jarrow at the time.

It is a small but important detail that Ellen Wilkinson, Jarrow's Labour MP who was instrumental in organising the march, was an ex-communist. She had been a founder member of the Communist Party in Britain in 1920, but after four years, disillusioned by its totalitarian ways, she turned her back on it to re-enter the democratic mainstream of British politics. She would become the country's first woman education minister, in Attlee's post-war Labour government.

Consensus and coalition

Europe was falling prey to two giants of evil, Stalin and Hitler, and to the new creeds of communism and fascism. Britain was a different world. The few native communists and fascists were noisy, but they were never more than fringe. Not a single fascist was elected to Westminster in a decade when they were triumphant in Italy, Germany and ultimately in Spain. Communist MPs could be counted on the fingers of one hand. In Britain, consensus and coalition were the order of the day.

So was social flexibility, although this should not be exaggerated. The top 1 per cent of the population was not as spectacularly rich as it had been before the Great War, when it owned 69 per cent of the nation's wealth. In 1936 the figure was down to 55 per cent, but most of the drop had not gone to the poor. Far from it, in fact. The drop for the wealthiest had been absorbed by the rest of the top 5 per cent, who in 1937 had 79 per cent of all wealth. The great majority of people in Britain had very little personal property at all. Some 8 million

NORTHERN MILL TOWN
A view of Colne in Lancashire shows the price Britain had paid for being the first workshop of the world. On this summer day in 1930 it was at least possible to look out across the town, which was more often obscured by smoke drifting from the factory chimneys. There was a meanness – to the barrack-like factories, the tiny terraced cottages, the filthy rivers and streams – that smacked of the elevation of profit above principle. D H Lawrence complained in 1930 that the industrialists in the 'palmy Victorian days' had condemned their workers to 'ugliness, ugliness, ugliness: meanness and formless and ugly surroundings … great hollow squares of dwellings … little four-room houses with the "front" looking outward into a grim, blank street …'

families, or three-quarters of the population, would have realised less than £100 had they sold all they owned. They were, to all intents and purposes, propertyless.

In Victorian days, industry had been the great wealth-creator, but that was no longer true. Four in five millionaires in the 1930s had made their money in commerce and finance. They were bankers, stockbrokers, insurers, shipowners, retailers, merchants. A third lived in London: the provinces no longer had as much clout. The public school stranglehold was firmer than ever. The great majority of Conservative MPs – and in the Thirties most MPs were Conservatives – came from public schools, as did 190 of the 271 top civil servants. Public schools produced more than three quarters of bishops, deans, high court judges and directors of the major banks. Nine in ten directors of the big railway companies were former public schoolboys, as were four in five senior managers in the steel industry. Very little changed over the decade. A study in 1931 showed that 524 of the 691 holders of 'high office' in church, state and industry were public schoolboys, with well over a third of them coming from just five schools: Eton, Harrow, Winchester, Rugby and Marlborough. The ratio had scarcely budged by 1939.

Nevertheless, Ramsay MacDonald's upbringing in poverty in Scotland did not prevent him becoming the most powerful man in the land. Philip Snowden, his chancellor, was born in a two-roomed hovel near Keighley in West Yorkshire, a weaver's son who became a viscount. The Liberal Rufus Isaacs was one of nine children of a Jewish fruit merchant from Spitalfields in London. Neither his class nor his religion prevented him from becoming the Marquis of Reading, ambassador to Washington and viceroy of India.

SOUTHERN STREETS
The narrow streets around Whitechapel High Street in London's East End had seen waves of Jewish immigrants. By 1938 a few Indians had arrived as well, like these smartly dressed young men. Although new houses were being built on greenfield sites out of London, slum clearance in cities was slow. Across the country, more than half a million dwellings were waiting to be demolished under the slum clearance acts, and another 350,000 'marginal dwellings' were slums in all but name.

THE HUNGER MARCHES

The Jarrow Hunger March is the unemployed crusade that has gone down in the collective memory, but in fact hunger protests were a feature of the 1930s as people marched on London from areas of high unemployment to ask, not for charity, but for the right to work to earn a living. None of the marches achieved their aim, but they did raise awareness of the problems faced in some parts of the country.

ACTIVE PROTEST

After its victory in the 1931 election, the new National Government immediately introduced the Means Test. This cut unemployment benefit payments for anyone who had some savings to fall back on, or relatives with funds who could help them. The result was that most people did not get the full unemployment benefit. The Means Test created fierce anger against the test and those who administered it, and above all against Ramsay MacDonald and the old Labour leaders, who were accused of class betrayal. A National Hunger March on London was organised in 1932. A million people signed the petition, carried by the 2,500 marchers, demanding the abolition of the Means Test. These men (below) marched down from Yorkshire; they were photographed at King's Cross station as they returned home that November. Even as late as February 1939, banners at a rally in Trafalgar Square (right) spoke of 'hunger' and 'starvation.' The difference in attitude can be seen in the faces: the smiles below hint at optimism that things will change; the grim faces opposite reflect the knowledge that they won't. The dole was just enough to keep body and soul together, and no more. Labourers in the country could eke it out by keeping rabbits and growing their own vegetables. In the industrial areas, there was little men could do other than scour coal tips for fuel. And the real hardship for many began when the full dole ran out after the 26 weeks for which it was payable.

'The men do not want charities. They want jobs.'

Ellen Wilkinson, MP for Jarrow, from *The Town That Was Murdered*,
an account of the Jarrow March published in 1939

THE JARROW MARCH
On the long trek down from Tyneside, the Jarrow marchers were fed and offered shelter by well-wishers along the way (left). The photograph above was taken as they passed through the village of Lavendon, near Bedford, some of the men playing mouth organs to keep up their spirits in the rain. On reaching London on 31 October, 1936, they were led through Hyde Park by the Jarrow MP, Ellen Wilkinson (top left). The marchers carried a petition begging the government to act over unemployment, which had reached a staggering 75 per cent in the town after the big shipyard, Palmers, laid the men off. The marchers gained much sympathy from the public and the press, for they conducted themselves with dignity and no hint of 'Bolshiness' (behaving like Bolsheviks) to frighten off the popular newspapers. But the shipyard stayed idle, apart from a little shipbreaking – sad work for men who had proudly built ships, not broken them up.

A VERY BRITISH FASCIST

It is ironic that the great extremist of the time, far from being radicalised in a slum, was a 6th baronet. Sir Oswald Mosley, Blackshirt leader and fan of Mussolini and Hitler, was born in 1896 to a wealthy family of country squires with an estate at Rolleston that employed 30 gardeners. The men in the family were traditionally boxers. They staged bouts in the ballroom, like Regency rakes. Following the tradition, Mosley was an accomplished boxer as well as a swordsman. During the Great War he had served in the trenches and in the Royal Flying Corps.

Mosley was first elected to Parliament in 1918, aged just 21, as Conservative MP for Harrow. Unhappy with the government's position on Ireland, he crossed the floor of the House to become an Independent. By 1924 he had joined the Labour Party. Elected Labour MP for Smethwick in 1926, he was hailed as the Party's golden boy, its most brilliant young member. Almost everyone, according to social reformer Beatrice Webb, thought of him as a future leader. Labour was a party of plebeians and plain men, she explained, and hitherto MacDonald had no competitor in 'personal charm and good looks … and the gift of oratory. But Mosley has all three, with the élan of youth, wealth and social position added to them.' He was a brilliant speaker and debater, he worked hard and he had ideas. But there was always a streak of impatience, instability and violence about him.

In 1930 Mosley was junior minister for unemployment under Jimmy Thomas, whom he despised. He wanted action and proposed a radical programme of public works to be financed by government loans. When MacDonald turned it down, Mosley resigned from the government and the Labour Party. In a fierce speech to the Commons on 29 May, he warned that if nothing was done Britain would sink to the level of Spain, a dreadful fate for a country that within everyone's lifetime had 'put forth efforts of energy and vigour unequalled in history'.

The New Party

Mosley's next move was to form his own political party – the New Party. At first its future seemed bright. Osbert and Sacheverell Sitwell joined, along with the young photographer Cecil Beaton, the left-wing Oliver Baldwin, Stanley's rebel son, and the equally leftist ex-Labour MP and Old Etonian, John Strachey. Literary figures who joined the New Party included Christopher Isherwood, whose Berlin stories inspired the musical *Cabaret*, and the diarist and diplomat Harold Nicolson. These were interesting men, but Mosley did not keep them for long. In April 1931, the New Party candidate Allen Young took 16 per cent of the vote in a by-election. By summer, Young and Strachey had left. Of 24 candidates fielded by the New Party in the general election of October 1931, only two managed to save their deposits. By April 1932 Mosley had formally disbanded the party.

He was, his friends thought, wildly impulsive and arrogant. They suspected that he would now 'play the He-man'. Beatrice Webb wrote that 'The British electorate would not stand a Hitler … Mosley has bad health, a slight intelligence and an unstable character. He lacks genuine fanaticism. Deep down in his heart he is a cynic. He will be beaten and retire.' She would turn out to be right. But for now, Mosley displayed a taste for street-fighting that echoed the fascists on the

FASCIST OFFENSIVE
Sir Oswald Mosley in full cry at a meeting in 1934 (near right), as membership of his British Union of Fascists (BUF) was beginning to build. His veneer of sophistication and stage presence made him seem more significant than he was. He had glamour and was a powerful orator, but he was too obviously a pale pastiche of Mussolini and Hitler – Malcolm Muggeridge called him 'the Lilliputian Führer'. Moseley's black-shirted admirers – seen here (far right) giving him the classic Nazi salute on 4 October, 1936, shortly before provoking the Battle of Cable Street – were almost comically theatrical, compared to the truly menacing Blackshirts and Brownshirts in Italy and Germany. Some of his women fans were photographed in their blackshirts, berets and A-line skirts while on parade in Liverpool in 1935 (bottom right). They have a slightly bashful air, as well they might. Mosley tried to exploit the political tensions thrown up by the slump, but the British Union of Fascists never came remotely close to power. It was all bark and no bite, and failed to attract the vast majority of the British public. Not a single BUF member entered Parliament.

Continent. He used the communists, who broke up his meetings, as an excuse for veering to the extreme right. Mosley said this 'forces us to be fascist', Nicolson noted in his diary. Uniforms were discussed. 'I suggest grey flannel trousers and shirts', said Nicolson. His notion of making them look like schoolboys did not go down well and he, too, was soon gone, to become a National Liberal MP.

Mosley visited Rome in January 1932 and met Mussolini. He was impressed. When he launched his new British Union of Fascists (the BUF) in October 1932, he issued members with sinister – but vaguely ludicrous – black shirts. Shirts were big with demagogues: Mussolini's followers were blackshirts, Hitler's were brownshirts. A little later, in Argentina, Peron's devotees were the Shirtless Ones.

Setting out his stall
Mosley's 'Mein Kampf' was *The Greater Britain*, a book he wrote in the summer of 1932. He argued that Britain was in crisis. If no action was taken, she would sink from imperial grandeur to decadent weakness, as Spain had done. The innate intelligence of the Anglo-Saxon race gave hope for the future. To exploit that superiority, Mosley would rule a well-disciplined state with a small cabinet. Parliament would survive, but with limited powers. Much of its work would pass

THE BATTLE OF CABLE STREET
Anti-fascist protesters put up barricades in Cable Street on 4 October, 1936, to prevent Mosley and his followers from marching through the East End of London (left). They clashed with police (above) and with Mosley's men in what was called the Battle of Cable Street. Most people, though, were utterly unmoved by extremists on Left or Right. They found the clenched fist salutes of the Reds as distasteful as the outstretched arms of the fascists. Moderation prevailed.

to 24 corporations, each representing a particular industry. Capitalism would remain, but under tight state direction. The aim was self-sufficiency in an imperial trading bloc. Cheap foreign imports would be banned, with British industry able to pay high wages and hire the unemployed. The powers and freedoms of trade unions would be curtailed. Women were to be encouraged to stay at home rather than compete with men for jobs.

All this was radical, but Mosley sought to soothe the public with his respect for tradition – the monarchy, Church and Empire – and for a time the BUF did not fare badly. By February 1934 its membership stood at 17,000 and this trebled to around 50,000 after Lord Rothermere's *Daily Mail* began to champion the BUF. It did not last. In June 1934, at a rally at London's Olympia, Blackshirt stewards brutally beat up some hecklers. The same month, Hitler's ruthless murders of his Nazi critics in the 'Night of the Long Knives' highlighted the dark side of fascism. Rothermere was no fascist, he was a reactionary Tory. He withdrew his support in July 1934 and within a year or so membership had all but evaporated, down to around 5,000.

The BUF staggered on thanks to Mussolini, who between 1933 and 1936 sent it some £60,000. The party campaigned in 1935 against British support for League of Nations sanctions on Italy over Mussolini's invasion of Abyssinia, but it cannot be said that Il Duce got much for his money. Mosley, remembering the humiliation of his New Party at the polls in 1931, put up no candidates at all for the 1935 election. Instead, he produced the rather lame slogan, 'Fascism Next Time'.

Anti-Semitism backfires

One of the New Party candidates in that disastrous election of 1931 had been a Jew – Kid Lewis, a welterweight boxing champion, who lost his deposit standing for his home constituency in Whitechapel. But gradually Mosley came to adopt an anti-Semitic stance that had more in common with German Nazis than Italian fascists. In May 1934 Jews were barred from the BUF. This struck a chord with some in London's East End, which by now had a large and not as yet fully assimilated number of Jewish immigrants – a third of all Jews in Britain lived in the East End. BUF members attacked Jews and their property amid considerable violence, most notoriously in the Battle of Cable Street on 4 October, 1936, when a march of 1,900 Fascists was blocked by tens of thousands of protesters. In the municipal elections of 1937, the BUF came second in a number of East End seats, but it was not close to winning in any of them.

The violence in London made people elsewhere more, not less, sympathetic to the Jews. The BUF obsession with 'the Jewish problem' alienated the vast majority of Britons, for whom the problem was non-existent. The troubles in the East End led the government to pass the Public Order Act in 1936. This banned political uniforms and gave the police powers to ban or re-route any provocative march they deemed might cause trouble. Young men who had welcomed the chance to march in BUF uniform and have a rumble with protesters found this amusement withdrawn. The party became smaller – and more middle-class – by the month.

THE COMMUNIST CONNECTION

For all the talk of 'Red Clydeside' and the 'little Moscows' in South Wales, the communists fared little better in Britain than the fascists. Party membership was around 7,000 for most of the Thirties, reaching a brief peak of 18,000 late in the decade. They were, though, very active. The propaganda in the party paper, the *Daily Worker*, embraced the arts and book pages, where films, theatre and writing were all seen in Marxist terms. It tried to appeal to the working man, with sports pages covering football and boxing, as well as the decidely non-Marxist 'Sport of Kings' – horse-racing. The party churned out pamphlets by the hundred thousand, which were sold on street corners by eager volunteers.

Communist Party membership represented only those who were willing to devote themselves to the cause. The number of general sympathisers, or 'fellow travellers', was higher and might have been greater still had the British Communist Party not been so slavishly under Soviet control. It raised so little money on its own behalf it became dependent on handouts from Moscow. This involved it in tortuous efforts to reflect Stalin's will, which in turn alienated patriotic British workers who were suspicious of foreigners.

Communist candidates were trounced in the 1931 general election, most of them losing their deposits. Later, they gained some useful publicity from the clashes with Mosley's Blackshirts. Moscow also moderated its hostility to Western governments as the increasing power of the Nazis in Germany forced it to seek allies in the West. The party only put forward two candidates at the 1935 election. One of them, William Gallacher, was elected for West Fife. This 'popular front' period, when the party relaxed some of its scorn for others on the left, saw it gain members but it never had any real hold on the working class.

Middle-class sympathisers

Intellectuals were altogether more susceptible. It was now that the Communist Party recruited three undergraduates at Trinity College, Cambridge: Guy Burgess, Donald Maclean and Anthony Blunt, later infamous as traitors. Burgess was the grandson of an admiral and an Etonian. He was a Gladstone Memorial Scholar at Trinity. Maclean's father was the president of the Board of Education when he went up to Cambridge in 1931. The other man in this little nest of spies was Kim Philby, who had gone up to Trinity in 1929. His father was St John Philby, an Arabist and adventurer, who was political adviser to Ibn Saud in Saudi Arabia.

The gullibility of apologists like the playwright George Bernard Shaw was astonishing. 'GBS' visited the Soviet Union in 1932, at the height of his fame. He was driven through Moscow and to selected parts of the countryside when farms were being turned into collectives by the state. 'Tales of a half-starved population dwelling under the lash of a ruthless tyrant' were nonsense, he later wrote in *The Times*. There were 'crowds of brightly dressed well-fed happy-looking workers'. Also, he added, 'in the USSR, unlike Britain, there is freedom of religion'.

Even as Shaw was writing such words, millions of Ukrainians were starving to death in a deliberate terror-famine. Requisitioning gangs, equipped with sounding rods, were swarming over sheds and cellars to see if peasants had held back some of their grain from the state. Tens of thousands were shot, and millions taken to labour camps in Siberia, where they died of cold, overwork and starvation. The equally gullible churchman Hewlett Johnson, the 'Red Dean', claimed in 1937 that

OVERALL PROTEST
The League Against Imperialism sets out its position in Trafalgar Square in August 1931. Little support was forthcoming. Britain was still the greatest imperial power in the world. The majority of Britons may not have been as proud of the Empire as they had been in the heyday of Victorian jingoism, but few were ashamed of it, either, and they had little time for the siren songs of crypto-communists like these. In reality, 'anti-imperialist' often meant 'Stalinist', and as such 'anti-imperialists' were inflicting inhumanities in Soviet Russia on a cold-blooded scale undreamt of in British colonies.

Soviet criminal camps were 'more marvellous than Canterbury Cathedral'. Yet the Soviet Commissar for Justice, Nikolai Krylenko, said that all verdicts in Soviet courts were designed to 'promote the prevailing policy of the ruling class and nothing else'. There was, he said, 'no difference' between a judge and a member of Ogpu, the political police. Krylenko's own trial followed in 1938. It amused Stalin to persecute the persecutors. It lasted 20 minutes, after which Krylenko was shot.

The mass murders in villages and work camps in the Soviet Union during the Thirties remain less notorious than the wartime Nazi concentration camps. Many on the left turned a blind eye. But the outlines were known. Independent-minded journalists like Malcolm Muggeridge exposed them in reports from Russia – and were expelled. Intellectuals who witnessed Communist Party tactics in the Spanish Civil War, like George Orwell and Arthur Koestler, became aware at first hand of the evils of Moscow-style communism. At show trials in Moscow, Henry Thornton and three other manifestly innocent British engineers working on a project in Russia for Metropolitan Vickers were accused of 'deliberately wrecking' the Soviet economy. Worse than this black comedy were the trials in which Party leaders pleaded guilty to working for British and French intelligence, and were then shot.

As the decade progressed, the British and French were becoming outnumbered in Europe by those living under dictatorships. It is only with hindsight that they can be criticised for not regarding the Nazis as the greater menace. In the pre-war period, far more died from bestial treatment by Stalin than as yet from Hitler.

THE GAME GOES ON

A GREAT BRITISH BATSMAN
Jack Hobbs (below) played his first game for Surrey in 1905. He was still going strong in the 1930s: 98 of his 197 first-class centuries – the highest total in the history of cricket – were made after he turned 40.

As ever, sport helped to keep minds off the evil doings across the water. The 1930s were a golden era for cricket. The London County Council had 350 cricket pitches, and a thousand clubs applying to use them. The game was even more popular in the North. The Roses matches between Lancashire and Yorkshire had a national following. Jack Hobbs, who was the first cricketer to be knighted, opened the batting for England in his last Test match in 1930, but he went on playing for Surrey until 1935, when he was well into his 50s. By then, he had scored 61,237 runs in first-class matches, a record that still stands. Hobbs and Herbert Sutcliffe were an unrivalled pair of openers, and all-rounder Wally Hammond was at his peak, scoring 3,000 runs in Tests against Australia. Hedley Verity set a first-class record in 1932 by taking all 10 wickets for 10 runs against Nottinghamshire.

BBC broadcasts of Test matches attracted huge audiences. 'Live' coverage from far-flung matches was enabled by telegrams sent from the ground detailing each ball bowled, which the 'commentator' used to describe the game. Celebrities and intellectuals had yet to pose as football fans. Cricket was the game.

The sensational cricket story of the decade was the MCC's 'Bodyline' tour of Australia in 1932–3. The MCC won the Ashes, but the Australians claimed that this was only because of dangerous bowling by Nottinghamshire fast bowler Harold Larwood. The English captain, D R Jardine, defended what he called 'leg-theory' bowling, insisting that it was fair. It was certainly effective: even the great Australian batsman Donald Bradman struggled to cope. Larwood was a

The great cricket story of the decade was England's victorious tour of Australia in 1932–3. The fast bowler Harold Larwood (left) was a phenomenon. He was only average height and build, but his pace, strength and near-perfect rhythm enabled him to bowl at over 90mph. Encouraged by the England team captain, D R Jardine, Larwood pitched the ball on the leg side, so that it rose sharply at the Australian batsmen. At the time batsmen were protected only by leg pads, with no helmet or body padding. As the struggling batsmen fended the ball off, a ring of English slips and other fielders gobbled up the catches. Jardine defended it as 'leg-theory' bowling. The Australians – outraged by the bruises Larwood inflicted and his large haul of wickets – called it 'bodyline' and 'brutality'. England won the Ashes and Jardine wrote a best-selling book about the tour (below), but the Australians complained so bitterly the government felt obliged to intervene. Jimmy Thomas, the Dominions Secretary, summoned MCC members to Downing Street. Cricket, he said, was the main sentimental link between Australia and the Mother Country and he urged them not to strain Anglo-Australian relations any further. As a result Larwood, a bowler whose brilliance had tamed even the great Donald Bradman, never played Test cricket again.

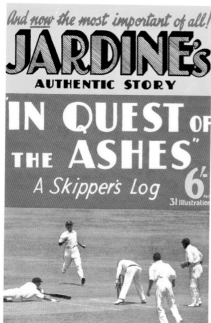

slender, almost slight figure, but he bowled with extraordinary power and pace. The Australians called his bowling 'preventable brutality' and threatened to call off the Ashes tours. Larwood was not selected when the Australians next toured England. He felt betrayed by the cricket establishment – with good reason.

Larwood was thus not part of the record-breaking team of 1938. In the Fifth Test against Australia at the Oval, in August 1938, England scored 903 runs for seven wickets declared. The margin of the win – an innings and 579 runs – remains another Test record. A 22-year-old Yorskshireman, Len Hutton, stayed at the crease for 13 hours to score his 364 runs. Don Bradman, Australia's captain, was the first to shake Hutton's hand when he broke the old record of 334, which had been held by Bradman himself. During the innings, Hutton ran six miles between the wickets, before eventually being caught. His score stood as a record until 1958 when Garfield Sobers hit 365 not out against Pakistan in Jamaica.

TEST MATCH
ADMISSION BY PAYMENT AT TURNSTILES
N 11 TO 15 WELLINGTON PLACE.
PLAY NOT GUARANTEED
NO MONEY RETURNED   3/-   PER DAY INCLUDING TAX

Despite the spread of cricket around the empire, the game in England was still firmly divided into 'Gentlemen' and 'Players', or amateurs and professionals. Separate dressing rooms were common. County sides were captained by amateurs and so was the MCC. Wally Hammond reverted to amateur status in 1938 to be able to captain Gloucestershire and England.

Sweepstakes and football pools

The arrival of two new forms of gambling gave the very poorest dreams of riches to keep them going. The Irish Sweepstake was started in Dublin in 1930 and soon became hugely popular with the British public. Public lotteries were forbidden in Britain (though clubs were allowed to run sweepstakes for members), but the Post Office could not stop people buying tickets in Dublin without censoring the mail. Over the decade, the Sweepstake took in more than £60 million, of which £14 million went to Irish hospitals and £2 million to the Irish government in taxes. Politicians in Britain were urged to copy it, but were nervous of antagonising Nonconformist voters implacably opposed to all forms of gambling.

Meanwhile, the football pools rocketed to popularity in Britain and by the late Thirties had overtaken the Sweepstake in the amount staked. The pools were based on guessing the football results, with each entry costing as little as a penny. Profits and overheads were deducted from the total wagered, and the remainder was distributed among the winners. A vast army of agents covered the country from town to village, distributing coupons and collecting takings. Most entries, though, came through the post. The volume was so huge that extra postmen were employed on Mondays and Tuesdays, when the new coupons were delivered.

CRICKET FANS
The appeal of the Ashes crossed all social, class and gender lines. Here, a party of Hampstead schoolgirls queue to get into Lord's for the second Test against Australia in 1938; they had been up especially early to be sure of a place. The long queues for each Test match confirmed the nation's love of this traditional sporting rivalry. Even non-cricketers felt personally involved, although it was not easy to be an England fan even then. The writer Robert Graves noted that 'ENGLAND IN PERIL' and 'CAN WE AVOID DISASTER?' were the usual newspaper headlines.

The pools were heavily advertised in the popular papers. They were also promoted on Radio Luxembourg and Radio Normandie, two commercial radio stations that got round the BBC's monopoly by broadcasting programmes for British consumption from abroad. The growth was startling: 10 million people were soon doing the pools, hoping that their 2s 6d stake would win them £22,000, equivalent to 100 years wages for the best paid manual worker. Queues built up in post offices as people lined up to buy postal orders. During the 1934–5 football season, at least £20 million was spent on the pools. A year later, that had doubled, and politicians and churchmen were fretting over the money wasted, in small but regular amounts, by families that could ill afford it.

A change of leader

It was a sign of Britain's underlying stability that there were just three prime ministers over this turbulent decade – the nation's closest allies, the French, could get through that many in a fortnight. Furthermore, the changeovers were smooth and crisis-free. In June 1935, Ramsay MacDonald retired and Stanley Baldwin,

THE IRISH SWEEPSTAKE
Tickets for the Irish sweepstake being delivered to the Plaza Cinema Hall in Dublin for the draw in October 1932. An ex-bookie had persuaded the Irish government to sanction the sweepstake in 1930 as a way to raise much-needed money for the underfunded Irish hospitals. It was first run on the Manchester Handicap, then in 1931 it was extended to three legendary British races: the Grand National, the Derby and, as here, the Cesarewitch. Millions of tickets were sold in Britain and America and soon the sweepstake was the biggest employer in Ireland after Guinness. The prettiest nurses in Dublin picked the winning tickets at a ceremony held three times a year in the Plaza Cinema Hall, which soon became a top tourist attraction in itself.

who had first become prime minister in 1923, returned to Number 10. Nothing stuck to 'honest Stan'. He liked to be thought of as a country worthy, torn from reading Wordsworth and going for walks in Worcestershire to do his duty for the nation. He was very much a part of Old England. He was Rudyard Kipling's first cousin, and his aunt was married to the pre-Raphaelite painter Edward Burne-Jones. He was a patriotic and generous man. In 1919 he had spent £120,000, a fifth of his fortune, on War Bonds and presented them to the government. The letter he wrote to *The Times*, suggesting that the 'wealthy classes' should follow suit, was signed 'FST'. He was then Financial Secretary to the Treasury, but no one realised it was Baldwin, as he intended. Only one person is believed to have followed his example. Baldwin called a general election in November 1935. The National Government was returned with a large, if slightly reduced, majority.

Signs of recovery

As the decade went on, the recovery was based on cars, bicycles, electrical goods and, from the mid-1930s, rearmament centred on the aircraft industry in Coventry and Bristol. People moved where the work was. The booming industrial estates at Slough, for example, sucked in labour from the Welsh valleys. The Midlands car, van and lorry plants attracted families from the North and Scotland.

Electricity was the key. The National Grid was all but complete by 1933, with new power stations connected by a grid of high voltage power lines. Electricity

GAME, SET AND MATCH
Fred Perry leaps the net after winning the men's singles final at Wimbledon in 1935. Perry, the son of a Labour MP, came into the game late. He was the world table tennis champion in 1929 and only took up tennis when he was 19. Between 1933 and 1936, when he turned professional, he won every major amateur title, including the US singles three times and the Australian and French championships. He was Wimbledon champion three times and the last British man to lift the trophy.

Swimming boomed in the Thirties, with smart outdoor Lidos being built. There were also big new road-houses with large swimming pools, which pulled in afternoon trade with huge notices inviting people to 'Swim, Dine, and Dance.' Here, Edyth Macready (right), the new Ladies' Diving Champion of England, makes a spectacular and graceful dive from the high board at Havre-des-Pas on Jersey.

continued on page 98

SCOUTING, RAMBLING AND THE YHA

These images capture the Thirties love of the great outdoors. Scouts in Scotland (above) pause on the slopes of Ben Nevis on a tour of the Highlands in 1938. The Lake District was popular with hikers: these two young women (bottom right) are admiring the view from the famous Wishing Gate at Grasmere in 1935. Earlier in the decade, ramblers assembled to support an Open-Air Charter to preserve public rights on roads and footpaths in 1932 (top right).

One organisation at the heart of outdoor pursuits was the Youth Hostel Association, founded in 1930. The idea came from the *Jugendherbergen* in Germany. It had spread to small groups like the Northumbrian Trampers' Guild by the late Twenties, and huts and shelters were made available in walking country like the Pennines and Lake District. The YHA opened its first permanent hostel at the City Mill in Winchester in 1931. The movement was a stunning success. The Harrow, Wembley and Watford YHA illustrates the growth. It was inaugurated in March 1936. On its first outing, 24 members went to Chorley Wood by train and walked back along the Chess valley to Latimer for lunch. In June, members noticed a large, empty house in the village of Ivinghoe in Buckinghamshire. Harrow YHA rented it for a nominal 5 shillings a year, volunteers renovated it and the hostel opened its doors at Easter 1937. By 1939, the YHA had 297 hostels and 83,418 members in England and Wales. Separate associations in Scotland, Ulster and Eire brought the total number of hostels in the British Isles to 397, with 106,000 members spending more than half a million nights in them.

Ramblers clubs sprang up across the country and a National Council of Ramblers was set up in 1935. Much of Britain was out of bounds, with bailiffs and gamekeepers keeping a close lookout for trespassers. Ramblers now lobbied for greater access and persuaded the Ordnance Survey to mark footpaths on maps to show where walkers had rights of way.

WHITE-COAT WORKERS

Women making radios in a clean modern plant in 1938. Conditions in the booming electricity-powered industries were better by far than anything that had gone before. The workers here all have the benefit of individual electric lighting to help them see what they are doing. Radio had moved rapidly since the first post-war crystal sets requiring complicated aerials and headphones. Valve sets with integrated loudspeakers came in. Many were powered by an accumulator – something like a car battery – that needed recharging from time to time, but by the Thirties there were also mains electricity radio sets. Reception was vastly improved, so that sound quality was excellent in all but the worst atmospheric conditions. Prices tumbled, too. Currys were selling two- and three-valve sets on hire purchase for one or two shillings a week. The number of radio licences, which stood at just 36,000 in 1922, had passed the 2 million mark four years later and reached 8 million in 1939.

output quadrupled in the 15 years leading up to the war, and the numbers employed in the electricity industry also soared to 325,000. The one house in three that was wired for electricity in 1930 had become two houses in three by 1939. The impact on industry was perhaps even more dramatic, as manufacturing was largely released from coal for their power needs. Factories powered by electricity were utterly different to the blackened buildings of old plants, with their belching chimneys and the sirens that sounded each shift. The fine new factories along the Great West Road into London had scarcely a chimney between them. They made the new products of the new industries: potato crisps, scent, toothpaste, fire extinguishers, bathing costumes.

The Hoover plant at Perivale was a symbol of this modernity, built in stunning Art Deco style. The factory was light and elegant, constructed of steel, glass and concrete, and set amid well-tended lawns and flowerbeds. The arterial road beside it carried the trucks and vans that supplied the factory with parts and then distributed its brand-new vacuum cleaners to the thriving markets of the Southeast. No railways, no coal, no noise, no smoke. Hoover boomed. In the very worst years of the Depression, between 1930 and 1935, sales of vacuum cleaners increased twelve times, rocketing up from 37,550 to 409,345. Other electrical appliances – refrigerators, cookers, heaters, radio sets, reading lamps – also brought work and good wages to those that made them and an improved quality of life for the families who could afford them.

Cars became another major new industrial employer. In 1924 Britain had produced 146,000 motor vehicles. By 1937 the half-million-a-year mark had been passed. The number had risen every year – even in the worst of the slump from 1929 to 1933. Cars brought vibrancy and good wage packets to Dagenham and also to the Midlands at Coventry, Birmingham, Luton and Oxford.

Advances in plastics and artificial fibres gave fresh impetus to chemicals. 'Rayon' and other yarn was used in clothing. Plastic, often as 'Bakelite', became a standard material for radio sets. ICI, the giant chemicals combine put together in 1926, did well across a wide range: fibres, synthetic dyes, pharmaceuticals, fertilisers. The industry was employing 100,000 by the time the war broke out.

Population and productivity

Changing demographics helped. A falling birth rate meant that the 15 to 64 age group was growing faster than the population as a whole. In mid-Victorian days, that group accounted for less than 60 per cent of total population. By 1937 it was within a whisker of 70 per cent. These were people at the peak of their producing and consuming powers, boosting both national output and consumption.

Technology gave another boost. Mass production revolutionised productivity in everything from cars to radio sets. Electricity not only spawned new industries, it transformed old ones. Electric coal cutters in the pits and power tools in engineering led to big rises in output. Credit instalment plans – better known as hire purchase, or the 'never never' – were another factor, making it easier for consumers to spend. J Gibson Garvie, the boss of United Dominions Trust, a major credit supplier, hoped that 'the principle of instalment-buying will eventually prove the spearhead of an advance to a fuller civilisation'. It was already producing an indebted one with 'repo' – repossession from families that could not keep up payments – increasingly common. Ellen Wilkinson, Labour MP for Jarrow, got a private member's bill through Parliament that meant defaulters were at least partially reimbursed for what they had paid out.

The thousand-odd chain stores built between the wars shrugged off the Depression. Marks & Spencers opened 129 brand-new stores between 1931 and 1935, and enlarged 60 more. Turnover, impressive at £2.5 million in 1929, grew tenfold over the next ten years. Most medium-sized towns now boasted a Marks and Sparks, a Sainsburys or Lipton's, and a Woolworths. Between them they made a big range of food, clothes and household goods readily available. It was the beginning of the threat to small grocers and traditional corner shops.

CARS FOR THE MASSES
Workers on an assembly line at the Morris car plant at Cowley in Oxford rub down the bodywork after its first coat of paint. Perhaps surprisingly, the Thirties were boom times for car factories. In 1919 there had been around 100,000 cars on the roads. Twenty years later, that had ballooned to 2 million. No longer was a private car an unimaginable luxury. The cost of an Austin Seven had fallen to £120 by the early Thirties, and small Morrises sold for between £100 and £200. Traffic lights, roundabouts and 'Belisha beacons' at pedestrian crossings were all introduced to help control the ever-increasing number of cars on the roads. Even so, road safety was an issue: the death toll was far higher than it is today, reaching 7,300 in 1934.

UNCERTAIN TIMES

On 20 January, 1936, wearing a floral dressing-gown, George V held his last Privy Council meeting in his bedroom at Sandringham. He could barely sign his name, and he soon lapsed into a coma. Rudyard Kipling had died shortly before. 'The King has sent his trumpeter ahead', they said. Lord Dawson, his doctor, issued a famous bulletin that read: 'The King's life is moving peacefully towards its close.' He would not last the night. George had come to the throne in 1910 amid a constitutional crisis. He not only steadied the ship with quiet dignity and compassion, but also steered the monarchy through the war-time storms that followed. His death would provoke an even bigger crisis for the royal family as his eldest son, Edward VIII, proved unsuitable to succeed him.

A GRAND DAY After tempestuous months for the monarchy – the death of George V, the abdication of Edward VIII – a girl tucks into cake on Coronation Day, 12 May, 1937. Her coronation teacup bears pictures of the new king, George VI, and his queen, Elizabeth.

THE ABDICATION CRISIS

F amously, George's last words were reported to be 'bugger Bognor', as in the seaside resort of Bognor Regis, but this is probably apocryphal. The new king's first action was a deliberate break with the past. 'I'll fix those bloody clocks', he said, referring to the clocks at Sandringham that his father and grandfather had kept on 'Sandringham time', half an hour ahead of the rest of the country. Edward ordered all the clocks in the house to be changed to GMT.

The new reign began with an ill omen. A funeral cortege took the body from King's Cross railway station to the lying-in-state in Westminster Hall. As the procession entered New Palace Yard, the Maltese cross containing the oldest crown jewel of all, St Edward's huge sapphire, was jarred loose and fell to the ground. The Grenadier Guards regimental sergeant major quickly recovered it. 'Christ!', said the new king. 'What will happen next?'

George V was dearly loved and deeply mourned. Almost a million people queued to file past the bier and pay their last respects. From Los Angeles, John Masefield, the Poet Laureate, cabled a sonnet:

'This man was King in England's direst need
In the black-battled years when hope was gone
His courage was a flag men rallied on
His steadfast spirit showed him King indeed.'

The new monarch was Edward VIII, known as David in the family while he was Prince of Wales. He was slender and blond, an 'adored Apollo' as a youth. He wore his uniforms well, and he was a good horseman and polo player, but there was also a fragility to his slight frame and a melancholy in his eyes and mouth hinting that, though he sought pleasure, he did not find it. But he was the symbol

A MUCH-LOVED KING
George V prepares to make his radio broadcast from Sandringham in 1933 (right). He had broadcast his first Christmas message in 1932, with a script written by Rudyard Kipling: 'I speak now from my home and my heart to you all; to men and women so cut off by the snows, the desert or the sea that only voices out of the air can reach them; to those cut off from fuller life by blindness, sickness or infirmity, and to those who are celebrating this day with their children and their grandchildren – to all, to each, I wish a happy Christmas. God bless you.' Although a dyed-in-the-wool conservative – his great passion was stamp collecting and he persisted with his beaver beard long after they had fallen out of fashion – he was broad-minded on many social issues and not afraid to embrace change. The nation celebrated his Silver Jubilee in 1935. His death at Sandringham in January 1936 touched the world. Thousands of schoolchildren sent messages of sympathy to his widow, Queen Mary. These boys at the Hugh Myddleton school in Clerkenwell, London (left), are observing two minutes silence as a mark of respect. The public were particularly touched by news from Tibet that the monasteries had spent a day in prayer for the King. According to the writer Robert Graves, the common refrain was that 'He was a good man and we shall miss him'.

of Young England, modern, racy, seen with jobless miners in South Wales and dancing the Charleston in Mayfair. He was always at odds with his father, and his natural charm and grace were in stark contrast with two of his brothers – the awkward, stammering Duke of York, and the plodding, witless Duke of Gloucester. So too, though, was Edward's selfishness and pleasure-seeking. He was obsessed with fashion, with jazzy socks, bright checks and large knotted ties, with 'smart nightspots, louche weekends, horseplay, jazz and jigsaw puzzles'. He had sympathy with the poor, but he spent his time with rich socialites.

Edward had enjoyed a love affair with Freda Dudley Ward, a married woman described as 'discreet, pretty … and pleasure-loving'. They had met during an air raid in 1918. By the Thirties the affair had turned to friendship, by in May 1934 when Mrs Dudley Ward rang St James's, as she often did, the telephonist was embarrassed: 'I have something so terrible to tell you that I don't know how to say it. I have orders not to put you through.' The prince had met someone else: a 37-year-old divorcée. She was still there when he became King.

THE PEOPLE'S PRINCE
A great throng of schoolchildren cheer the Prince of Wales during his visit to Ponciau Banks recreation ground, lighting up a dreary day in North Wales in May 1934. The prince was hugely and deservedly popular with the British public. For all his natty dressing and night-clubbing, his visits to depressed mining and factory towns showed real interest and sympathy for the working class. That is why when the abdication crisis broke in 1936, this man was on his bicycle in Downing Street lobbying to keep Edward as king.

Indiscretion and informality

Edward's short reign was to be described as a 'blaze of indiscretion'. The cause of the fire was an American woman, Mrs Wallis Simpson. She had been born Bessie Wallis Warfield in Baltimore, but was always known as Wallis. After an unhappy first marriage, she had moved to Europe and married Ernest Simpson. The marriage failed, through his infidelity. It was, ironically, in the house of Ernest Simpson's sister that the prince had first met Mrs Dudley Ward.

Wallis had now, as Stanley Baldwin put it, 'stolen the fairy prince'. She was chic rather than feminine, half artifice – she spent hours on make-up – half steel. Part of her attraction to Edward was that she showed him no deference, as her home-grown rivals did. She was quite willing to bully him, getting him to paint her toenails or fetch her cigarettes – and he adored her. He wrote her little notes, calling himself her 'small boy'. He neglected his duties to see her, and even showed her confidential government papers. His private secretary was appalled at her influence: 'before her the affairs of state sank into insignificance ... every decision, big or small, was subordinated to her will'.

A bitter dispute between the generations was at the bottom of this and other rows of the time. The Prince of Wales and his father had more or less detested one another. Court life was dull, but it was solid and respectable. It was taken as read that the nation expected solidity in their king. David had sown his wild oats. Now that he was Edward VIII he must set aside his pleasures, as Prince Hal had put away Falstaff when he became Henry V. But he showed no signs of doing so. He hired a luxury yacht, the *Nahlin*, for a reputed £250,000 and spent the summer of 1936 cruising round the eastern Mediterranean with Mrs Simpson and friends. 'Vive l'amour!', the Yugoslav papers cheered as the *Nahlin* sailed down their coast.

There was homegrown gossip, too. On one occasion the King had his brother, the Duke of York, deputise for him at the opening of an Aberdeen hospital, while he went to a nearby railway station to meet Mrs Simpson. The staff at Balmoral were flummoxed at the way formality crumbled. Curtsies were 'scarcely required',

CELEBRITY COUPLE
The new king, still uncrowned, on holiday with Wallis Simpson in the summer of 1936. All the world seemed to know that Edward was in love with Mrs Simpson – except the British public. The American and Continental papers were full of the couple's affair. In those more deferential days, the British press breathed not a word of it. Many in London society, though, were aware of the situation and knew that a constitutional crisis would follow if he insisted on marrying the twice-divorced American.

ceremonial door openings and calls to meals were scrapped or sloppily performed. No word of such doings appeared in the British press, though *The Times* dropped hints that a sovereign 'should be invested with a certain detachment and dignity … which are not so easily put on as a change of clothes'. The affair might be common knowledge among journalists and in London society, but it was also etiquette that, since the royals could not comment or reply to stories, it was unfair to mention their foibles. The last time this rule had been broken, Robert Graves wrote, had been by a sporting newspaper in the 1880s when the new king's namesake, Edward VII, had been Prince of Wales. There was 'nothing whatever between the Prince of Wales and Lillie Langtry', the newspaper announced, adding a week later: 'Not even a sheet.'

The American press was full of the couple. Never, it was said, had there been such a human-interest story since Mark Antony had sacrificed an empire for Cleopatra. The *News Chronicle* ran a front page story that Mrs Simpson was going to Ipswich to get a divorce. It did not say why this American woman and her soon to be ex-husband merited page one. The judge at the hearing was startled to find his court full of American reporters.

It was the bishop of Bradford, Dr Blunt, who finally broke the story to the British public. Dr Blunt planned to use a diocesan conference to urge the King to take the Christian aspect of his forthcoming coronation seriously. The King needed 'faith, prayer and self-dedication … if he is to do his duty properly'. The bishop hoped the King realised that he needed divine grace, but wished 'he gave more positive signs of his awareness'. On 30 November, following his usual practice, Dr Blunt sent a copy of his speech to the *Yorkshire Post*, blissfully unaware of what he was about to stir up. The next day, the *Post* splashed his comments and the dam burst. Rumours flew. Mrs Simpson was to be made Duchess of Lancaster, it was said, before marrying the King.

Taking sides
Baldwin discussed the matter in Cabinet. He sounded out the dominion governments, for the monarch was the formal political link between Britain and the empire. They found a twice-married woman, who was also a commoner and a foreigner, too much to stomach. 'Most ordinary people were for the King', said Graves. 'Most important people were against him.' Churchill and Beaverbrook

were the core of the 'king's party', though it was said that they supported him as much to get rid of Stanley Baldwin as from personal loyalty. Mosley was for him. The King himself flirted with a morganatic marriage: he would marry Mrs Simpson without making her queen and any children would drop any claim to the throne. Baldwin would not have it. The king's wife must be queen, and her issue heirs to the throne. 'God save the King', loyalists shouted, 'from Mr Baldwin.'

The country was in the hands of Old Men. They saw the set Edward moved in as spivvy and flash, and resented the way he was so contemptuous of the values of their generation. Baldwin was almost 70, deeply conservative and a champion of morality in public life. His own son, Oliver, had rebelled against him in much the same way as Edward had with his father. Oliver Baldwin had become a socialist MP and refused to speak to Stanley for the best part of a decade. He then fell under Mosley's influence and was one of the founder members of the New Party in 1931. Cosmo Lang, the archbishop of Canterbury, was 71, a Scot who had been a dean of divinity at Oxford. He did not mince his words when he said it was strange that the King 'should have sought his happiness in a manner inconsistent with the Christian principles of marriage ... within a circle whose standards and ways of life are alien to all the best instincts and traditions of his people'.

Palace officials were hostile. The King rarely went to church, they whispered, he disliked protocol and showed it in public. He had replaced some of them with younger men and had even removed the herd of royal goats from Windsor Great Park and exposed them to the common gaze of visitors to the Zoo.

Mrs Simpson removed herself to France. The A-word, 'Abdication', was mentioned in the *Daily Mail*. Communists and Fascists found common cause for once. 'There is no crisis in all this business for the working class', said Red leader Harry Pollitt. 'Let the king marry whom he likes.' Mosley placed his Blackshirts behind the King because, it was said, the King was a Nazi sympathiser.

On 10 December it was all over. Baldwin read out the King's statement of abdication in the Commons. Edward gave a farewell address to the nation on the BBC, then he slipped across the Channel, on a dark warship, as Duke of Windsor. He was succeeded by his brother, the Duke of York, who came to the throne as George VI. It was an excuse for some Shakespeare: 'Now is the winter of our discontent made glorious summer by this son of York.'

THE NEW ROYAL FAMILY
After dining with his brother, who had just abdicated, the new King George VI returns to his home in Piccadilly in December 1936 (above left). The contrast between the two brothers could not have been greater. Where Edward was outgoing and flamboyant, George was shy, with a stammer that he strove to overcome in public speaking. Where Edward lived the high life and had affairs with married women, George married young and had a happy family life. This photograph of his wife Elizabeth, then Duchess of York, and daughters Elizabeth and Margaret Rose was taken in March 1935, before the abdication crisis arose. George neither wanted nor expected to become king, but he accepted the challenge as his duty.

THE BBC – A NEW BRITISH INSTITUTION

It was fitting that the King bade his people goodbye on radio, for this was the giant medium of the age. The new valve sets with built-in speakers, either powered from the 'mains' or 'wireless' and powered by an accumulator, all but did away with the old crystal sets with headphones. They cost more – in Currys the cheapest 2 and 3 valve sets were £3 or so, against £1 for a crystal set – but they were only a couple of shillings a week on hire purchase. The best were sleekly designed in Bakelite, the new form of plastic, and were the work of famous designers like Serge Chermayeff and Misha Black.

The BBC had a monopoly of home broadcasting, with the only competition coming from the Luxembourg and Normandie commercial stations in Europe. These were profitable concerns, making their money from advertisements. Their ads for hot drinks – the Ovaltineys, the Horlicks Tea Hour – were known to all. In contrast, the BBC was funded by the radio licence of 10 shillings a year. With more than 8 million issued by 1939, this was enough to fund the organisation in style. In 1932 it moved its headquarters to Broadcasting House in Portland Place, a fine art deco building, honeycombed with broadcasting studios. It was said to have eight light bulbs for every person who worked there. In its maze of dark internal passages, with 800 doors leading off them, they were needed.

The BBC's output was largely highbrow at first, with classical music and heavy drama. The BBC Symphony Orchestra started in 1930 under Adrian Boult and became the main orchestra for the annual 'proms', the famous promenade concerts later broadcast from the Albert Hall, with talks by heavyweight musicians like the conductor Malcolm Sargent. There was also a very popular series called 'This Symphony Business', in which a self-confessed philistine allowed himself to be charmed by serious music. It supported British composers such as Constant Lambert and William Walton, and the last works of Frederick Delius. The BBC Theatre Orchestra made its first broadcast in July 1931, and was followed before Christmas by the BBC Chamber Orchestra.

By the late 1930s more varied light entertainment with dance bands, popular singers, comedians and sport was in the ascendant with radio audiences. Chamber music was at the bottom of the ratings. More women listened to the radio than men, and more old people than young. Peak times were at midday and in the early evenings. The regional studios provided talent from across the country. Kathleen Ferrier made her singing debut in Newcastle in 1939. Wilfred Pickles auditioned in Manchester. They soon moved to 'the Smoke', as smog-ridden London was known. 'All the good men go to London', Pickles noted. 'I wonder why?'

Changing audience habits

Serial plays were broadcast on Sundays – *The Count of Monte Cristo* and *Les Misérables* were two of the most popular – and gained such large audiences that clergymen complained when they coincided with Evensong. Not only were their

congregations diminished, they said, but they themselves missed out on episodes. The regular 'Saturday Evening Music Hall' had so many listeners that it affected other forms of entertainment. Cinema and theatre proprietors were most annoyed by 'Band Wagon' at 8.15pm on Wednesdays, as their midweek takings were dropping by as much as a third. Women's Institutes, evening classes and the like rearranged their meetings to Tuesdays and Thursday.

It was the annual Royal Command Variety performance that was the real bugbear for show business. It was so popular on the BBC that cinemas, music-halls and theatres ran to near-empty houses. The BBC at first agreed to pay a large sum to charity for the broadcasting rights. This was good for charity, but it did not tempt the audience away from their radio sets. Complaints multiplied, and in 1938 the BBC was forced to abandon the broadcasts altogether.

Sometimes radio had the opposite effect and saved a show. Once a fortnight the BBC ran 30-minute extracts from plays and musicals and it was often on the strength of this that people went to see the whole show in a London or provincial theatre. *Me and My Girl* was a classic example. It was the Christmas show at the

NEWS FROM THE RING
Still black with coal from working in a South Wales pit, Richard Farr, the brother of heavyweight boxer Tommy Farr, listens anxiously to the radio with his family for news of Farr's world title fight against Joe Louis in 1937. Louis, known as the 'Brown Bomber', was unbeaten world champion for a record 12 years, inflicting 25 defeats on his opponents – including Tommy Farr. Through radio, sports fans were able to listen at home to live coverage of their favourite sport. At first, because of pressure from evening papers, the BBC did not broadcast results. But the rule was relaxed, and by 1939 most important sporting events were being covered.

ENJOYING A HIT
Actor and director Lupino Lane fronts the
chorus line in *Me and My Girl,* alongside
musical comedy star Teddie St Denis, at
the Victoria Palace, London. The show had
been about to close after just a short run
at the Chelsea Palace at Christmas 1937,
when the BBC broadcast Lane singing
'The Lambeth Walk'. The song became a
huge hit and not just in Britain. The dance
spread to America, reversing the usual
westward flow of music, and soon even
the Czechs were forgetting their political
troubles with its infectious gaiety. The
show had a reprieve on stage, transferring
from Chelsea to Victoria, while its famous
hit song sold more records and sheet
music than anything since 'Yes, we have
no Bananas.'

Chelsea Palace for 1937 and its run was almost over when the BBC broadcast an
excerpt, which included 'The Lambeth Walk' sung by Lupino Lane. He played a
cockney who inherited an earldom without abandoning his old ways, and
delighted the titled guests at a smart dinner party with an old London song:

> 'Any time you're Lambeth way, Any evening, any day
> You'll find us all doin' the Lambeth Walk.'

A dance was invented to go with it, which took off after the Duke and Duchess of
Kent were said to have danced it. It was a welcome home-grown change to the diet
of imported rumbas and tangos.

As far as the public was concerned, the BBC could do little wrong, but it was
too successful by half as far as the popular press was concerned. The *Radio Times*,
giving details of the week's programmes, reached a circulation of 3 million, much
to the chagrin of magazine publishers. At first, the BBC was careful not to
broadcast the result of big horse races like the Derby for fear of hitting evening
newspaper sales. Listeners heard the pounding of hoofs in the Derby, and the roar
of the crowds, but the results were kept quiet until the 6pm watershed when the
evening papers would no longer be harmed. This rule was gradually relaxed for
sporting events, but no news broadcasts were made between midnight and 6pm,
due to pressure from press barons anxious to preserve a news monopoly for their
papers. The only exceptions were events of national importance: the crash of the
R101, the death of George V, the political crisis of 1938.

Spreading its wings

The BBC helped to stitch the far-flung dominions and colonies together. The Empire Service was started in 1932. It later became the World Service. The first foreign language broadcasts were made in Arabic in 1938. European services began on the eve of the war, in German, French, Italian, Spanish and Portuguese as well as English. They would prove critically important in counteracting German – and Soviet – propaganda. Another area where the BBC shone was in its schools broadcasts, which were a great success. By the end of the decade, 11,000 elementary and secondary schools were listening in to teaching programmes.

The great sporting events became enshrined in radio programming: the Oxford-Cambridge Boat Race (which was so popular the phrase became rhyming slang for 'face'), the FA Cup Final, the Grand National, Wimbledon and cricket Test matches. Remembrance Day also drew huge audiences, and so did the King's Christmas Day message, inaugurated by George V in 1932.

The popular daily round-up show, *In Town Tonight*, began in 1933. Alistair Cooke began presenting *The American Half-Hour* in April 1935, a forerunner of

'OUR GRACIE'
Gracie Fields sings to construction workers at the Prince of Wales Theatre in London after laying the foundation stone in 1937. She was the one new variety star of the decade. With her Lancashire accent, her humour and unquenchable optimism, she was as far removed from Hollywood slickness as it was possible to be – and the nation loved her for it. She was born in Rochdale and was a child performer before becoming the top music-hall talent in the country, singing songs both comic and sad, and appearing in many films and royal command performances.

his record-breaking *Letter from America*. Two hugely successful radio shows were *Bandwagon* with Arthur Askey, which began in 1938, and ITMA – *It's That Man Again* – starring Tommy Handley, which started in 1939. By then three quarters of all households had a radio. The audience almost doubled over the decade.

Radio helped to give Britain the strong and unforced sense of identity that foreigners remarked on. It was natural that Edward VIII's abdication message was carried by radio, so that the whole country could hear it. And Prime Minister Neville Chamberlain used it to announce to the nation the declaration of war with Germany on 3 September, 1939.

The start of TV

The world's first regular television service began from the BBC studios at Alexander Palace on 2 November, 1936. Sir John Reith, the BBC's great founding father, refused to be televised as part of the opening ceremony. Television, he said, was an 'awful snare'. It was certainly modest enough in its infancy. 'Ally Pally' was in North London, and only those within 35 miles of it could pick up the signal. The first sets had tiny 10-inch screens and cost £100 – as much as a small car. By the outbreak of war, only 20,000 homes had TV sets. Actors were paid less than radio rates for television appearances because the audience was so small. But the fledgling service did its few viewers proud. For its first outside broadcast, on

FOOTBALL ON TV
Arsenal players crowd round the camera after playing in the first football match to be filmed for television anywhere in the world, on 16 September, 1937. The game was of no importance – Arsenal first team were playing their own reserves – but the occasion was a milestone in television history. TV sets were still rare and expensive. Only a few thousand viewers watched the historic grainy pictures, but they gave an unforgettable glimpse into popular broadcasting in the future.

12 May, 1937, it televised George VI's coronation procession – around 10,000 were able to watch it. Then it was at Wimbledon for the tennis in June. It could only cover the finish of the 1938 Boat Race, but it kept viewers up to date with the race by moving model boats on a mock-up of the course. A few weeks later it was at Wembley for its first FA Cup Final.

Richard Dimbleby – father of David and Jonathan – was at Heston airport on 30 September, 1938, for BBC radio and television to report on Chamberlain's return from Munich. TV also gave advance warning of the Second World War. A Mickey Mouse cartoon was showing on 1 September, 1939, when it was suddenly blacked out: it was feared that German bombers might home in on the signal. The television service was suspended for the duration of the war. When it restarted on 7 June, 1946, the very first programme shown was the interrupted Mickey Mouse.

The television service had only three announcers in the decade. Leslie Mitchell was the first in 1936 – and he was later the first on ITV, in September 1955. Elizabeth Cowell was a tall and imposing lady. The third, Jasmine Bligh, was the strikingly beautiful niece of the Earl of Darnley, and a descendant of Captain Bligh of the *Bounty*. The ladies wore evening dress to make announcements after 6pm. They had to learn their lines to read the news – no autocues in those days – and theatrical training helped. Jasmine Bligh was famous for re-opening the television service after the war: 'Good afternoon, everybody', she said. 'How are you? Do you remember me?' Despite its small budget, the service had style in plenty.

FIRSTS IN THE AIR AND AT SEA

In hindsight, more important than the Abdication was a little noticed event at Eastleigh aerodrome, now Southampton airport, in March 1936. A new fighter aircraft, the Supermarine Spitfire, had its first test flight. The pilot was Captain 'Mutt' Summers, and it handled so perfectly that on landing he told the engineers: 'Don't touch anything.'

The Spitfire was the final masterpiece of the designer R J Mitchell. He was dead within a year, but his creation has a touch of immortality to it. The public first saw it at the Hendon Air Display in July 1936, and were at once entranced by the grace of its unmistakable elliptical wings, and the growl of its Rolls-Royce Merlin engine. It was more complicated to build than the Hawker Hurricane, whose maiden flight preceded it by four months. More Hurricanes than Spitfires would fight in the Battle of Britain, but it was the Spitfire that caught the heart and the mind. The first order for the RAF was for 310 aircraft, at a cost of £6,033 each, and the first one rolled off the assembly line in May 1938. When production ended 10 years later, 20,351 Spitfires had been built. One had flown at 606mph, within a whisker of 1,000km/h; another had reached an altitude of 51,550 feet.

Pilots adored the Spitfire. Mitchell's brief was to create a fast monoplane fighter that exploited the power of the Merlin engine to the full, while retaining the manoeuvrability of the RAF's existing biplanes. He succeeded triumphantly, producing a very forgiving aircraft. One Spitfire lost its propeller in a high speed dive, yet the pilot was able to glide it for 20 miles back to his home airfield.

The term 'Spitfire' was used by the Elizabethans to describe a fiery or zestful temperament. It was suggested by a director of Vickers-Armstrong, Supermarine's parent company, who called his fiery young daughter 'a little spitfire'. Mitchell himself thought it was 'just the bloody stupid sort of name they would choose'.

'It would shudder and shake and rock you from side to side, but if you handled it properly it would never get away from you. There are many pilots alive today who owe their survival to this remarkable quality in the Spitfire.'

Jeffrey Quill, Supermarine Spitfire test pilot

Luxury liners

Another great maiden event took place in Southampton at the end of May. The transatlantic liner *Queen Mary* sailed on her first voyage for New York. As with the Spitfire, built in response to the German fighter plane, the Messerschmitt 109,

MAJESTIC LINER

The *Queen Mary*, almost completed, is admired by a crowd at Clydebank near Glasgow in March 1936 (below left). The new Cunard ship was a symbol that the worst of the depression was over, and that trade and travel had begun to pick up. The rivalry between the great French, German and British transatlantic liners was intense. Their passage times to and from New York were published in the popular papers, and much national pride was tied up in them. The crossing on the *Queen Mary* was truly luxurious for those who could afford it. These passengers (right) are dining in the splendid cabin class restaurant during the liner's maiden voyage from Southampton to New York. The radiating light on the map at the far end of the dining room pinpoints the ship's position as she steams at speed across the North Atlantic. The liner sailed into New York at dawn. These passengers (below) are up early to see the dramatic Manhattan skyline come in to view as the *Queen Mary* prepares to dock at the end of her first transatlantic crossing.

the *Queen Mary* was in part a response to the German ocean liners *Bremen* and *Europa*. The hull was laid down by John Brown's yard on Clydebank in December 1930. Work stopped after a year when Cunard, her owners, were hit by the depression. The government agreed to loan them enough to complete building her,

continued on page 120

THE PURSUIT OF SPEED

A love of speed and world speed records marked the Thirties. The 'Triple Crown' embraced the land, air and water speed records – and Britain held them all.

RECORD-HOLDERS

Sir Malcolm Campbell makes a record attempt to beat his own land speed record at Daytona in the USA in 1933 (left), reaching an official speed of 273mph. He passed on his passion for speed to his son, Donald, seen here (right) at the wheel of *Bluebird*, shortly before it was shipped to the USA for that record attempt. Sir Henry Segrave (below) held the land speed record before Campbell. He is seen here travelling at more than 100mph on the Brooklands circuit in 1930. In June that year he was killed in his boat *Miss England* while breaking the water speed record on Windermere. 'Did we do it?' he asked his rescuers. They nodded, and he died. The following year, George Stainforth broke the world airspeed record, flying at 407.5mph in a Supermarine S.6B seaplane, ancestor of the Spitfire, at Lee-on-Solent.

A SPEED STAR AND HIS CAR
Malcolm Campbell poses with
his improved *Bluebird* in
January 1935. The machine had
2,450 horsepower and
Campbell would soon use all of
that to become the first man to
break through the 300mph

barrier on land, hitting just over
301mph at Bonneville Salt Flats
in Utah in 1935. For his early
land speed attempts, he drove
on the Pendine Sands in
Carmarthenshire. On one
occasion his car almost sank in
quicksand and he transferred to

salt flats in America. He
reached his fastest speed on
water, 141mph, in 1939.
   Campbell named all his
racing cars and speed boats
Bluebird after the symbol of
unattainability, a tradition
continued by his son Donald,

who would follow in his steps to
hold both land and water speed
records. Donald died when his
turbo jet-powered hydroplane
flipped over on Coniston Water
in 1967, as he attempted to
become the first man to break
the 300mph barrier on water.

STEAM POWER

Another speed record came to Britain in 1938. On 3 July train Driver Duddington, seen here (above) with his fireman, steered steam locomotive *Mallard* – the Gresley A4 Pacific no. 4468, as every train spotter knew – to 126mph. It was the fastest speed achieved by steam power anywhere in the world. The streamlined locomotive was almost brand new and belonged to the LNER, the London & North Eastern Railway. It achieved its record speed on the downslope from Stoke Summit to Peterborough on a London-to-Newcastle run. Although it maintained 126mph for just 185 feet, the Doncaster-built Mallard did manage to keep up an average speed of over 120mph for five miles on this stretch, all the time hauling a seven-coach train. *Mallard* remained in service until 1963, clocking up 1,426,260 miles. No steam train has ever beaten its proud speed record.

and her slightly younger sister ship *Queen Elizabeth*, on condition that they merged with the rival White Star Line. *Queen Mary* was launched in September 1934, shooting down the slipway faster than expected and almost grounding on the opposite bank. By the time the fitting out was completed, she had cost £3.5 million – enough to buy 580 Spitfires. It was said that Cunard wanted to call her *Victoria*, but when they asked George V for permission to name her after Britain's 'greatest queen' he replied that his wife, Queen Mary, would be most pleased. She journeyed to Clydebank to launch her namesake.

The ship's gross tonnage was 80,744. This would have made her the world's largest liner, but the French had increased the tonnage of her rival, the *Normandie*, from 79,000 tons to 83,000 by enclosing a passenger area on a boat deck. The *Queen Mary* had her revenge, though. Her captain, Sir Edgar Britten, had to slow her on the last day of her maiden crossing when she ran into thick fog. But she soon captured the Blue Riband from *Normandie* with an average speed of 30.14 knots westbound and 30.63 knots eastbound. Fitted with new propellers, the *Normandie* reclaimed the prestigious record in 1937, but the *Queen Mary* won it back in 1938 with a record that stood until 1952.

Her lines were traditional and her décor restrained, but she was luxurious through and through. Woods from different parts of the empire were used in her public rooms and staterooms. The indoor swimming pool took two decks in height. She had a nightclub, library, nursery, even a ship's kennel. A model of the ship moved on a large map of the North Atlantic in the first class dining room to show her current position. In the air, then, and at sea, Britain still had industrial genius. It was to be tested all too soon.

STEADYING THE SHIP

George VI worried lest the abdication crisis should cause the 'whole fabric' of the monarchy to 'crumble under the shock and strain of it all'. It was more robust than he thought. Only five MPs supported a Republican motion in the Commons, though one Tory thought that a hundred might have done so on a free vote.

The date of the coronation remained unchanged on that fixed for the absent Edward VIII – 12 May, 1937. References to him were taboo, though some banners in the East End defiantly read 'God Bless our King and Queen AND the Duke of Windsor'. The event was a gigantic celebration, a last hurrah, it seemed, as dark deeds spread on the Continent. Most of the crowned heads of Europe or their heirs apparent attended, though not the King of Italy, whose new title of Emperor of Abyssinia the British did not recognise. With unintended irony, Spain, in the throes of its civil war, sent a Republican minister.

After the ceremony, a crowd of Cup Final proportions – 100,000 or so – gathered outside Buckingham Palace. The Royal Family appeared on the balcony four times. In the evening, the King made a broadcast committing himself to serve the nation, his speech having only a trace of his stammer and shyness. It rained, so there was no dancing in the streets. No disloyal demonstrations were recorded that day anywhere, although in Dublin the IRA blew up a statue of George II.

HISTORIC OCCASION

The balcony of Buckingham Palace after George VI's coronation at Westminster Abbey. Queen Mary, widow of George V, is in the centre, flanked by the new King and Queen, with the young princesses, Elizabeth and Margaret, also wearing little crowns. A smiling Princess Elizabeth seems to take the event calmly and confidently in her stride. The abdication of her uncle meant that she was now heir to the throne. The BBC covered the coronation procession on TV, the first live outside broadcast in the world. The ceremony took place on 12 May, 1937, the same day that had been fixed for Edward VIII, who was now to spend his life abroad as the Duke of Windsor. A thousand special trains carried people to London from across the country for the celebrations. The decorations in Selfridges store on Oxford Street were so magnificent that an Indian rajah bought them to take home with him to embellish his palace.

The village tradition of celebrating coronations with gusto continued, though the squire was often missing now – done for by the agricultural depression – and his place was taken by the local vicar or doctor or the ranking retired army or naval officer of the neighbourhood. Peels were rung on the church bells in the morning. After the service, the strong Coronation ale brewed by many local breweries was drunk. Children danced round maypoles plaiting red, white and blue ribbons to the tune of 'Come, Lassies and Lads'. The afternoon was given up to village sports, tug of wars, tip and run cricket, and band races, where contestants had to play an instrument as they ran. A feast was held, followed by fireworks in the evening, torchlight processions and a bonfire.

A State Banquet was held at the Palace next day, to more cheering crowds and balcony appearances. On 19 May the new King and Queen drove to the Guildhall for lunch with the Lord Mayor. A grand review of the Fleet was held at Spithead later in the month. Eighteen other navies sent warships. The King sailed round the lines of ships in the royal yacht, and boarded the Flagship to order rum to be broken out: 'Splice the mainbrace!' The BBC had commissioned a former naval officer, Thomas Woodrooffe, for live commentary on the illumination of the fleet that night. Unfortunately, he enjoyed the ship's hospitality a little too much and was rather 'tired and emotional' by the time he was called on to broadcast at 10.45pm. 'The whole fleet is lit up', he rambled. 'I mean lit up with fairy lamps. It's fantastic … it's fairyland … When I say lit up, I mean outlined with tiny lights …' Then the illuminations were switched off. 'It's gone! It's gone! There's no fleet. It's disappeared …', cried Woodrooffe. 'There's nothing between us and heaven. There's nothing at all.' The BBC engineer mercifully faded him out.

The new Royal Family proved to be very popular. A favourite newsreel showed them at the Duke of York's Camp for Boys. The King, who always supported the scouts and guides, was seen leading them in 'Under the Spreading Chestnut Tree', singing and acting out the words by spreading his hands, touching his chest then his head (for 'nut') and branching his arms for 'tree'. He was relaxed, dressed in an open-necked shirt, the Queen was hatless, and the two princesses – adored by all – were in blouses and skirts. The lack of pomposity was beguiling.

A disappointing end

As to the Duke of Windsor, he married Mrs Simpson in a quiet wedding at Candé in the Loire in France on 3 June, 1937. Some at home remained attached to him, and bitter with Baldwin and the Church. Compton Mackenzie, the Scot who was to write the glorious comedy *Whisky Galore*, took up the cause of the 'King across

the Water' as passionately as if he was Bonnie Prince Charlie. But *The Times*, Church House and the other high places of the establishment continued, Malcolm Muggeridge noted, to treat the Duke with 'that frigid, calculated hatred which the English upper classes reserve for those they have unremuneratively adulated'.

The Duke and Duchess of Windsor visited Germany, ostensibly to study its social services, and met with Hitler in person. The meeting was ill-advised, adding fuel to simmering accusations of pro-Nazi sympathies. The Duke was subsequently persuaded to give up public life and live quietly.

George VI turned out a fine king. There are few grounds for thinking that the Duke of Windsor would have done better, but his behaviour over the abdication was faultless. He made no attempt to divide the country by capitalising on the great reservoir of public goodwill he had built up. But it was a sad end to a gilded youth. He had hoped to be 'Edward the Innovator', but could credit himself with only two changes: inaugurating the King's Flight of aircraft, and allowing the Yeomen of the Guards to shave off their beards. He was best known, perhaps, for the distinctive 'Prince of Wales' checks and for the 'Windsor knot' in ties. The relaxed style that he brought in proved lasting. Gentlemen began wearing corduroy trousers and jackets, previously the preserve of rustics. Overcoats became less formal, single-breasted and loose-fitting with Raglan sleeves. Young men about town picked up his old army officer's trick of wearing a silk handkerchief tucked into a shirt cuff. Spats disappeared and sandals flourished.

Baldwin bows out

The Coronation was Baldwin's swansong. There had been a half-hearted campaign against him by the Left with the slogan 'BMG' – Baldwin Must Go – but it was difficult to turn 'Honest Stan' into a hate figure. He managed to get through the crises – the Depression, national strikes, the abdication, the outbreak of the Spanish Civil War – and he knew when it was time for him to go. He saw George VI crowned, having brought him to the throne, and wisely decided to retire in the coronation glow. He became an earl, and retired to Worcestershire.

His successor as prime minister was Neville Chamberlain, lacklustre son of Joseph, the fiery Victorian premier. Neville had been a sisal planter in the West Indies before coming back to become Lord Mayor of Birmingham. He had gained his reputation as Chancellor of the Exchequer. He was brisk, businesslike and unremarkable, with bushy eyebrows and a drooping, old-fashioned moustache. His Cabinet had two former foreign secretaries, Sir John Simon, who replaced Chamberlain at the Treasury, and Sir Samuel Hoare, who had mishandled diplomacy over Mussolini's invasion of Abyssinia – now Ethiopia – and was rewarded for his blunders with the Home Office.

The new War Minister, a critical post in troubled times, was Leslie Hore-Belisha. He had been an effective and lively transport minister, and he did the best he could to modernise the army in the face of reactionary generals who were fonder of the horse than the tank. One general who was not hidebound, the commander in chief in India, Sir Philip Chetwode, complained that 'the longer I remain in the Service, the more wooden and regulation-bound I find the average British officer'. The manual *Cavalry Training* devoted 23 pages and 12 plates to exercises with the sword and lance. Armoured cars were dealt with in an aside: 'The principles of field operations in Cavalry Training (Horsed) are in general applicable to armoured car regiments.' It was not a good omen.

'HONEST STAN'
The traffic stops for Stanley Baldwin as he walks from Downing Street to the House of Commons to succeed Ramsay MacDonald as Prime Minister in June 1935. He had been in Number 10 before, arriving unexpectedly in 1923, and his time in office had included the General Strike in 1926. He served as lord president of the council in MacDonald's National Government. This time he would be in office until 30 May, 1937. He steered the country and the royal family through the abdication crisis, then stood down on a high note after George VI's coronation. Baldwin projected himself as a plain, sound, straightforward man. He had great tactical skills in surmounting crises with 'the least possible disturbance to himself, his party and the country'. In domestic politics he was shrewd and sensible. But he ignored warnings of the growing menace of the Nazis and German rearmament, and kept Winston Churchill in the wilderness. As the news from Europe darkened, Baldwin was not the only one in Britain who thought it was time for him to go.

A TASTE FOR ART AND LITERATURE

The British read as never before. Book sales rocketed almost fourfold in the decade. They reached 26 million in 1939, when public libraries reported almost 250 million book borrowings. Mobile libraries reached remote villages, and 'tuppenny libraries' were attached to tobacconists, sub-post offices and chain stores like Boots. Allen Lane began publishing Penguin paperbacks in 1935. The first two were Ernest Hemingway's *A Farewell to Arms* and *Ariel*, André Maurois' biography of Shelley. They cost 6d a copy, the same as a packet of cigarettes. Penguins were followed by the more educational Pelicans.

Readers did not shun the gathering political clouds. Penguin Specials were published on the important questions of the day. Book Clubs flourished, most famously the Left Book Club, founded by the publisher Victor Gollancz in May 1936, soon to have 60,000 members. The dandyism of the Twenties gave way to social concern. The 'new poets' – W H Auden, Stephen Spender and Cecil Day Lewis – 'got in touch with reality' with verses on electricity pylons, and were on the left. George Orwell, an unequalled essayist, lived down his Eton schooldays by writing and literally being *Down and Out in London and Paris*, and getting to grips first-hand with slums in *The Road to Wigan Pier*.

Murder, she wrote

People read for pleasure as well as duty, of course. Murder mysteries and detective stories reached their height. Some of the best-sellers were American, like Ellery Queen, but the natives were not outclassed. Dorothy L Sayers wrote with panache and style, creating Lord Peter Wimsey as her hero, and perfecting the English village setting in her bell-ringing tale, *The Nine Tailors*, in 1934. Agatha Christie's immortal spinster, Miss Marple, was equally at home in St Mary Mead. Miss Marple first appeared in 1930, in *Murder at the Vicarage*. Christie gave more exotic locations to Belgian detective Hercule Poirot, her other great creation, with *Murder on the Orient Express* in 1934 and *Death on the Nile* two years later.

It seemed surprising that two Englishwomen of such impeccable background should have been so at home with crime and murder. They were, however, racier than their readers knew. In her private life, Agatha Christie had divorced her first husband, a rarity at a time when divorce was still frowned upon. Her second husband was the renowned archaeologist Sir Max Mallowan. Dorothy Sayers was a blue-stocking – she had achieved a first in modern languages at Oxford – who had an illegitimate son and, almost as shocking, had worked in advertising. Both women, though, were devout. Sayers was a great Christian apologist, writing the BBC series *The Man Born to be King*, and translating Dante's *Inferno*.

In literature, D H Lawrence died in 1930. The Sitwell brothers and sister spun fashions in music, pictures and interior design. Osbert was a novelist and satirist with a showman's gift for publicity. Sacheverell was a romantic poet and expert on baroque art. Edith was a talented poet who turned to prose in the Thirties.

WELSH WORDS
Browsers at the annual Welsh Book festival in 1936 (top right). Wales retained a strong sense of its own identity. Welsh was still widely spoken and read, and Eisteddfods and other Welsh festivals were well supported. But there was little demand for self-government, despite South Wales being hit harder by the depression than almost any other region of Britain. Bilingual teaching and the disestablishment of the Church of Wales removed two major grievances. The nationalists were bookish folk, professors or students who wanted to revive Bardic culture, not agitators. Some Welsh lecturers did try to set fire to an RAF depot in protest at the desecration of local beauty spots, but there was nothing to compare to the violence of the IRA.

BOYS AND BOOKS
A group of schoolboys select books at the London County Council school library in Rotherhithe (bottom right). The raising of the school leaving age to 15, which the government had hoped to enact in 1931, was delayed by the financial crisis. The principle was re-introduced in the Education Act of 1936. It should have been implemented in September 1939, but this time the war intervened. By 1938, almost two-thirds of all children over the age of 11 were in secondary modern schools. Grammar schools took fee-paying and scholarship pupils. 'Direct grant' schools also took a percentage of scholarship pupils, in return for government grants. University education was still rare. In 1938 only 2 per cent of 19-year-olds were in full-time education.

CREATIVE MINDS

The ballerina Margot Fonteyn, photographed in 1937 (left). She spent her whole career with the Royal Ballet, creating many roles with Ninette de Valois and Frederick Ashton as choreographers. The sculptress Barbara Hepworth is seen here with her 'Mother and Child' (bottom left). She and her husband, the painter Ben Nicholson, were members of 'Unit One', a group of abstractionists who set themselves up against the 'unconscious school' of Expressionism. Stanley Spencer (below) was never part of any movement, a reason perhaps why he was so underrated, an eccentric who tackled unfashionable religious subjects with powerful originality.

The British had a particular genius for detective stories. Agatha Christie (top right) created two immortals in Hercule Poirot and Miss Marple. She also wrote plays, like *The Mousetrap*, and her novels begged to be filmed. The portly and good-humoured G K Chesterton (far right, below) created another memorable character in the detective-priest Father Brown. He was also a fine biographer and poet. H G Wells (far right, top) published *The Shape of Things To Come* in 1933, urging people to confront fascism before it was too late. Daphne du Maurier (right, below) was the beautiful daughter of the actor-manager Gerald du Maurier. She was a brilliant romantic novelist, with a splendid sense of plot and character. Several of her bestsellers, including *Jamaica Inn* (1936) and *Rebecca* (1938), became successful films.

IMMERSED IN ART
Two of the Sitwells – the poet Edith and her brother, the novelist and writer Osbert. With their other brother, Sacheverell, they were the children of Sir George Sitwell, an eccentric landowner who lived at Renishaw Hall in Derbyshire. Osbert was a fine short story and travel writer, with a mordant and satirical wit. Edith was an elegiac and romantic poet, who introduced jazz and dance rhythms into her work. Sacheverell was inspired by Baroque architecture. The press paid the trio great attention in the Thirties, and the Sitwells set fashions in music and interior design.

P G Wodehouse's characters – Lord Emsworth, Gussie Fink-Nottle, Bertie Wooster and Jeeves, his immortal butler – were still going strong. The classic *Right Ho Jeeves* appeared in 1934. Wodehouse described his work as 'a sort of musical comedy without music and ignoring real life altogether'. Frank Richards entertained children with his tales of Billy Bunter of Greyfriars School, as well as readers of *The Gem* and *The Magnet* comics. Arthur Ransome's classic *Swallows and Amazons*, telling of children's adventures in boats in the Lake District, was followed by a string of others. Ransome's professional and personal background was more exotic than his young readers might have realised. He had been a foreign correspondent for the *Manchester Guardian* in revolutionary Russia, and he was married to Trotsky's secretary.

The most original artist of the day was the social and sexual eccentric Stanley Spencer, who grew up in Cookham, a sleepy village by the Thames. Drawing on his experiences as a medical orderly in the Great War, he painted the haunting images of army life in the Sandham memorial, a powerful tribute to the fallen. In utter contrast, the fat and powerful women and lascivious little men he painted had something autobiographical about them. L S Lowry was painting his distinctive pictures of Lancashire industrial towns, in greys and blacks and brilliant whites, with stick figures beneath the smoking chimneys and blackened brick mills.

The sculptor Jacob Epstein caused a stir in 1931 with his large marble of a pregnant woman, 'Genesis'. It was, the *Sunday Express* declared, 'so gross, obscene and horrible that no newspaper has ever published a full picture of it.' The publicity did the exhibition the power of good, persuading thousands to pay their shilling for entry, though it was noted that many were so bashful that they averted their eyes in front of the statue. The younger sculptors, Henry Moore and Barbara Hepworth, were starting their careers.

Art Deco was the iconic architectural style of the age. Buildings included the abstract concrete Penguin Pool at London Zoo and striking new Underground stations in London, of which Arnos Grove was the best known.

A HOME FOR PENGUINS
The much-visited Penguin Pool at London Zoo was designed by Berthold Lubetkin. He left Soviet Russia for Paris, where he was influenced by Le Corbusier, before coming to London to set up his design company, Tecton. After his famous work at the Zoo in 1933, he designed a block of high-rise flats, Highpoint I in Hampstead, that was praised for giving a sense of real quality to high-rise housing. His Finsbury Health Centre was another landmark building.

THE SHADOW
DESCENDS

A ghastliness was loose in Europe, the writer Aldous Huxley said, 'an invisible vermin of hate, crawling about looking for blood to suck'. Hitler's lust for power and violence had been clear from the Night of the Long Knives in June 1934, when the SS – Hitler's personal bodyguard under the command of Heinrich Himmler and Reinhard Heydrich – had murdered hundreds of influential Nazis, including his rival Ernst Rohm. Now, in defiance of the Versailles Treaty, Hitler was openly rearming Germany. In March 1936 he sent troops into the demilitarised Rhineland zone. Then, in October, he established the Rome-Berlin 'Axis' with Mussolini's Italy, creating a fascist bloc in the heart of Europe.

TEST DRILL During the last days of peace in 1939, office workers practise evacuating to their air raid shelters. The government feared that real air raids, when they came, would create mass panic.

THE LOOMING WAR

The Japanese war in China began in July 1937. The invaders were in Peking (Beijing) by August. The British ambassador to China was wounded in his car, but the incident was hushed over. By September, the Japanese were in Shangai. In December, they broke into Nanking (Nanjing), the Chinese capital, in scenes of horrific mass rape and murder. They pushed on 500 miles up the Yangtse Kiang river past Hankow in 1938, and also occupied Canton in the South. China was too distant to cause much of a stir in Britain, but it should have set loud alarm bells ringing. Hong Kong and Malaya were uncomfortably close to the newly aggressive Japanese, while Burma and even India were not that far away.

The government response was appeasement – what the minister Oliver Stanley said was 'peace with as little dishonour as possible'. It was a popular policy, for all the warnings that 'mere cooings' would not placate the 'monster of German militarism'. For many, Hitler seemed a lesser menace than Stalin. The mass killings in Soviet Russia were concealed – only the perceptive realised they ran into the millions – but Stalin's show trials of 'Trotskyites' were another matter. There was revulsion when Marshal Tukhachevsky and seven other generals were shot. The marshal had been at George V's Jubilee in 1935 and was much admired.

By contrast, Hitler appeared sane. To rearm and to send troops into the Rhineland were widely seen as understandable and the Germans' own business. George Orwell felt that Middle England – the 'huge untouchable block of the middle class and the better off working class' – was patriotic to the core. If the country was in acute danger, they would rally to its defence. Otherwise, though, they did not feel that anything that happened abroad was any of their business: 'after all, England is always in the right and England always wins, so why worry?'

The German terror-bombing of the town of Guernica caused outcries and there was popular support for the Republican side in the Spanish Civil War. Captain 'Potato' Jones was hailed a hero when he ran his steamer past the fascist blockade to sail a cargo of potatoes into Bilbao for the starving citizens. But the only decisive action taken by the government followed the sinking of merchant ships bound for Republican ports by 'unknown' submarines. This was thought a slight to British naval prestige. Anthony Eden, the Foreign Secretary, called a meeting at Nyon in Switzerland. An agreement was made with the French and Italians to patrol the Spanish coasts to protect shipping. The sinkings stopped.

The far-sighted and the men in power

A few saw the future and were afraid. The diplomat Robert Vansittart warned that Britain was incapable of checking Japan 'if she really means business and has sized us up, as clearly she has done'. He said that 'by ourselves' – meaning without the Americans – 'we must eventually swallow any and every humiliation in the Far East'. Vansittart also feared a catastrophe if Britain remained weak in the face of the German menace. He had personally met Hitler and his henchmen, and had no illusions. Neville Chamberlain, on the other hand, had plenty. In January 1938, he had Vansittart removed as permanent undersecretary at the Foreign Office and left in a backwater. His replacement, Sir Alexander Cadogan, was grey and bland.

VOICE IN THE WILDERNESS
Winston Churchill laying tiles on the roof of a cottage on his estate at Chartwell in Kent in February 1939. He was a bricklayer, too, with an honorary Union card to back his claim, building walls to burn off the energy that he was prevented from putting to the public good by his banishment to the back benches. Churchill would much rather have been fixing the country's defences and armed forces. From as early as 1934, he warned time and again that 'Germany already has a powerful, well-equipped army, with an immense reserve of armed, trained men ... two years from now the German air force will be nearly 50 per cent stronger than our own, and in 1937 nearly double ...' Little or no notice was taken. Memories of the Great War left little appetite among the public for talk of more war, and the politicians in charge reflected that mood. He railed against Baldwin and then against Chamberlain, Baldwin's successor as Prime Minister, but they were in power. At the time Churchill was regarded by many as a warmonger, not as the all too accurate prophet that he turned out to be.

'… the trouble is, we are so damned weak.
It is Baldwin who has reduced us to this
shameful condition …'

Winston Churchill, speaking in 1936 on Britain's failure to respond to the growing strength of Germany's armed forces

Churchill was indefatigable in his warnings of Nazi danger, and his demands for rearmament. Most people thought him brilliant but unsound. He was remembered for the Dardanelles disaster in the war, for changing parties twice, for championing Edward over the abdication. Lloyd George agreed that he had a powerful brain, but added that it was prevented from running true by a 'tragic flaw in the metal'. Baldwin said that the good fairies at Winston's birth had given him daring, imagination, energy and courage. Then the bad fairy had spoiled it by denying him wisdom. Asquith had said of him that he had 'genius without judgment'. The charge stuck. The Tory R A Butler, who was at the Foreign Office before the war, described him as the 'greatest adventurer of modern political history' – and a 'half-breed American'. Churchill ran Chartwell, his home in Kent, like a miniature of Blenheim Palace, his birthplace. He created lakes, waterfalls and fishponds, he built his own walls, he painted, and he ate and drank as lustily as he hunted and rattled out the articles for newspapers which helped him to stay solvent.

CRAVEN 'A'

Always cool, smooth and easy on the throat

DRINKING AND SMOKING

Pints are pulled in a typical Thirties pub. A remarkable fall in drunkeness went with a fall in crime. The British had long been hard drinkers. Drink-related offences, though, fell from 52 per 10,000 inhabitants in the decade before the Great War to just 12 in the Thirties. Beer production fell over the same period from 34 million barrels a year to just 13 million. Seebohm Rowntree, the chocolate manufacturer and veteran philanthropist, was astonished to note the new soberness in York. 'One may pass through working-class streets every evening for weeks', he said, 'and not see a drunken person.' The Mass Observation project looked at drinking habits in Bolton. Only a third of adults made a regular weekly visit to a pub. Even on a typical Saturday evening, pub-goers accounted for only one in seven of all adults. A growing number of people smoked, though. Back in 1914, the British were smoking just over 2lbs (1kg) of tobacco a head per year. They had doubled that to 4lbs by 1938. Spending on tobacco soared from £42 million in 1914 to £294 million in 1939. Some of that rise was due to higher taxes. But advertisements – like this one for Craven 'A' (above) – and images of the leading man lighting cigarettes in countless films helped to boost cigarette sales, especially to women.

Neville Chamberlain was in utter contrast. With his reedy voice, self-satisfied smile and moral prissiness, he was said to be 'every inch the political haberdasher'. He wore an old-fashioned wing collar, black jacket and striped collar (so, sometimes, did Churchill, but he also often swapped them for a boiler suit) and was seldom seen without his umbrella. His views were stilted and narrow. The Americans were 'a nation of cads', the Russians were 'semi-Asiatic', the French couldn't keep 'a secret for more than half an hour, nor a government for more than 9 months'.

Neville had none of his father's eloquence and drive – Joseph Chamberlain had been the powerful colonial minister at the turn of the century – and his close colleagues were no better. At the Treasury, the lawyer Sir John Simon was known as a 'snake in snake's clothing', a man who had sat on the fence for so long, Lloyd George remarked, that some of it had entered his soul. Sir Samuel Hoare had been a prominent advocate of appeasement when at the Foreign Office, though he was strongly in favour of penal reform when he moved to the Home Office and was an early and persuasive opponent of capital punishment. Sir Thomas Inskip, the minister responsible for the coordination of Britain's defences, had 'little ability, less power and no perceptiveness'.

To make matters worse, none of Chamberlain's underlings stood up to him and this played to his vanity. One of his officials said that he set himself up on a pedestal, there to be 'adored, with suitable humility, by unquestioning admirers'. He was needled by the least criticism or mockery. He harassed his ministers. Anthony Eden believed that 'au fond', in his heart of hearts, Chamberlain had 'a certain sympathy for dictators, whose efficiency appealed to him'.

He was a bad judge of character, strikingly naïve in his trust that Hitler was a man of his word. His desire to have 'no more Passchendaeles', no more Great War-style massacres, was laudable. But what if the Germans wanted them? He thought that peace could be maintained by righting the wrongs of the Treaty of Versailles. He failed to see that Hitler was half-gangster, half-warlord, and utterly bound up in himself. Neither did he woo potential allies. He kept the French at a distance, and made no serious attempt to shift the Americans from isolationism.

Chamberlain was astonished when his Foreign Secretary, Anthony Eden, resigned. Eden was young, handsome, impeccably dressed, the son of a baronet with a fine war record. It was less clear at the time that he was also highly strung and subject to mood swings. The Nazis disliked Eden on sight – a 'notorious firebrand' – and he had as little time for them. At first, though, he had agreed with Chamberlain on appeasement. Then he vacillated. He was, Richard Crossman said, that 'peculiarly British type, the idealist without conviction'. On 20 February, 1938, he resigned, not because he was viscerally against appeasement, but because he thought Chamberlain was too accommodating to Mussolini.

Edward Wood, the third Viscount Halifax, replaced Eden. He was lofty in both height and demeanour, a sincere high churchman, and undoubtedly brave. He had been born without a left hand, but this did not stop him from hunting every Saturday that he could. Hindu terrorists had bombed his train while he was viceroy of India. He went on calmly reading a book of theology, remarking later that he was 'inured to that kind of thing by the Cona coffee machine always blowing up'. Halifax was conciliatory in India and he brought that attitude to Europe. But he had not come across anything like the Nazis and found it difficult to see them as they really were. 'An earnest and honest fellow', Beaverbrook said, 'not quite stupid, but inexperienced in worldly affairs.'

TIME FOR A BREAK

It was easier and easier to 'get away from it all'. The British had long been pioneers of mass tourism – Thomas Cook had invented it. Now, in June 1936, the first Butlins Holiday Camp opened at Skegness. It was sited rather unpromisingly on 200 uninviting acres of turnip fields by the grey waters of the North Sea.

Billy Butlin had begun by running stalls at travelling fairs, like his mother before him. He noticed that the growth of charabancs meant that more and more people were looking for their entertainment on the coast. He leased some sand dunes at Skegness, at first to develop an amusement site. Inspiration for the holiday camp came from a miserable holiday he spent on Barry Island, locked out of his B&B all day in the rain – the standard practice for seaside landladies.

FAMILY HOLIDAY
Campers at Butlins Holiday Camp in Skegness in 1938 make use of a communal hot water tap for brewing tea. Holiday camps were not new. A few companies, trade unions and charities ran them for employees, union members, the poor and convalescents. But Billy Butlin was the first to build a commercial holiday camp offering

all-in holidays. Meals in modern restaurants, sports and entertainment were included in the price, under the enthusiastic supervision of 'Redcoats'. The camp at Skegness was an instant success, and Butlin soon opened others at Clacton and Filey. Butlin and his camps caught the communal spirit of the British, and brought out their ability to laugh at themselves.

Butlin designed his camp to amuse and entertain whatever the weather. There was no need to sit on the chilly beach: the sea, he shrewdly realised, was not an essential part of a seaside holiday. Work began in September 1935, and he almost ran out of funds over a bleak winter. His plans were ambitious. He wanted 600 chalets, with electricity, running water and 250 bathrooms, a Viennese dance hall, fortune-tellers' parlour, a theatre and recreation hall. The camp sported a gym, a swimming pool with cascades and a boating lake. He had the grounds landscaped and filled with tennis courts, bowling and putting greens, and cricket pitches.

This was luxury for people who might not have electricity or a bathroom at home, and it was at a price that working people could afford. All-inclusive, with three meals and entertainment thrown in, it cost from 35 shillings a week (£1.75). There were teething problems in plenty, but people loved it. Capacity at Skegness was doubled and redoubled until it could take 10,000 holidaymakers. A second camp followed at Clacton in 1938, and work started on a third at Filey in 1939.

Butlin built up loyalty by issuing special enamel badges to each camper for the duration of their stay. The badge gave readmission to the camp if they went out. Campers kept their badges from earlier holidays, and proudly wore them all on a ribbon like campaign medals. They were well-made, too, by jewellery makers in London, Dublin and Birmingham. Butlin's staff, the smartly turned out Redcoats, were unmistakable and added to the colour and panache of the camps.

There were also holiday camps for the serious-minded. People at 'Left camps' spent hours in earnest political debate. Amateur dramatics, highly popular in the thirties, were the staple of drama camps. The routine at music camps began with physical jerks at daybreak. Individual practice on an instrument filled in the time between breakfast and lunch. Organised games or a walk led to tea-supper, and an impromptu concert in the evening.

The physical exercises at the camps reflected a broad 'keep fit' movement. *The Times* urged in November 1936 that a great national effort should be made to

SEASIDE BREAK

Not everyone was enamoured of the new holiday camps – thousands preferred to stick with the traditional seaside holiday. Britain's big beach resorts boomed in the Thirties as never before or since. And Blackpool was the most popular destination of them all. Here, Blackpool's famous sandy beach has all but disappeared beneath the crowds one fine day in 1932 (left). The holiday-makers in deckchairs (above) are enjoying a snooze in the Blackpool sun in 1939. On Bank Holiday Monday in 1937, more than 500,000 visitors descended on the town, in 50,000 cars and coaches and 700 trains, 425 of them Bank Holiday 'specials'. Well over 20 million people were going to the seaside each year and Blackpool was clocking up 7 million overnight visitors a year.

'improve the physique of the nation'. A fund was started in memory of George V to provide playing fields in the big cities. Women flocked to join the League of Health and Beauty, which ran PE classes. 'Fitness' had originally meant 'fit for military service' and there was a martial aspect to the health cult on the Continent. But where Mussolini was photographed jumping over fixed bayonets, exercise for British politicians did not go beyond a little gentle fishing and a round of golf.

THE AGE OF THE CAR

There had been more motorcycles than cars in 1920, but motorcycle numbers peaked in 1930, then fell by a third over the decade as more people found they could afford a car. The cost of an Austin Seven fell to £118 in the decade and the number of car owners passed 2 million. The 'Big Three' car-makers – Ford, Morris and Austin – were building more than half a million cars a year between them by 1937, and 400,000 people were working in the industry. Vauxhall was growing rapidly in Luton with the Light Six and Big Six – its Bedford trucks, which had a quarter of the van market. Vans and lorries were taking a sizeable share of the retail goods and factory supplies that had once been carried by goods trains.

One result of the growth in car traffic was urban ribbon development. The car spurred house-building on arterial roads and along the by-passes built around congested areas. They were soon lined with houses, shops and petrol stations. This was most noticeable on the outskirts of the cities, particularly in the Southeast. Extensions to the London Undergound and the electrification of the Southern Railway also led to road after road of new housing in places like Morden. Advertisements on the tube urged people to 'Stake your claim at Edgware'.

Almost 3 million houses were built in the Thirties as pebble-dash suburbs grew around the cities. Even in 1932, one of the worst years of the slump, more than 200,000 new houses went up. Many families who had lived cheek by jowl in crowded rooms now had a house of their own with a garden. It had always been an English dream to have a house and garden, and this meant that cities sprawled outwards more than Continental ones with their big apartment blocks. Cheap cars and new private bus services made development along the main roads practical. They also caused monster traffic jams. 'Road houses' were another sign

THE FAMILY HOME AND CAR
The Arsenal and England fullback Eddie Hapgood waves goodbye to his family as he sets off for training in 1936. The vast bulk of the 2.5 million new homes put up between the wars, like the Hapgood's, were built by private developers and not by councils or corporations. The houses were good value and usually solidly built. A new 'semi' could be bought for £450, with a deposit of £25 or so, plus a mortgage at 4.5 per cent. Almost all had electricity and a front and back garden. Pebble dash, 'Tudor' beams and leaded windows added a little individuality. 'Ribbon development' and 'bungaloid growth' were much criticised at the time, but Thirties suburbs have worn well.

of the love affair with the car. They were large and strikingly designed inns, part bar, part restaurant, part entertainment complex. Couples drove out to them to eat and drink, dance, play tennis and swim in summer – and stay overnight with few questions asked. The Great West Road into London had road houses every mile or two with big signs inviting people to 'Swim, Dine and Dance'.

These new suburbs had instant chain stores to cater for them: W H Smith, Sainsbury's, Dewhurst butchers, Express Dairies, MacFisheries, Burton's tailors, big banks, a building society. The houses, often half-timbered with elaborate ridge tiles and porches, cost up to £1,000, and were aimed at people on incomes of around £10 a week. Cartoonist Osbert Lancaster described them as 'By-Pass Variegated' and lampooned them mercilessly: 'some quaint gables culled from Art Nouveau ... twisted beams and leaded panes of stockbroker's Tudor ... a white wood Wimbledon Transitional porch making a splendid foil to a red-brick garage vaguely Romanesque

> The developers have ensured that 'the largest possible amount of countryside is ruined for the minimum of expense.'
>
> Osbert Lancaster, *Daily Express* cartoonist

in feeling'. He added that they did 'much to reconcile one to the prospect of aerial bombardment'. This was unfair – the houses were comfortable and generally well laid out, with gardens and a sense of space – but the sentiment was echoed by John Betjeman in his celebrated 1937 poem:

'Come friendly bombs and fall on Slough!
It isn't fit for humans now,
There isn't grass to graze a cow ...'

Slum clearance and new estates

New tenements were built in cities under slum clearance projects. They had broad paved courtyards, where children could safely play, and were a vast improvement on the slums they replaced. The man behind the slum clearance schemes – and the 1935 Housing Act, which laid down enforceable housing standards for the first time – was Lord Kennet, who had lost an arm manning a gun turret as a volunteer in Zeebrugge in 1918. He had been a vigorous minister of health in MacDonald's National Government. He believed in gardens and allotments – 'an Englishman's house is his castle, and his spade and hoe must have their castle too' – and in the use of gas and electricity in place of coal, anticipating the clean air acts.

The design of new estates, though, increased the cleavage between classes. 'Zoning' under the Town Planning Act of 1932 meant that land was developed at one, eight or twelve new houses to the acre. The size of plot made a great difference to the value of each house and thus segregated residents by income.

The Campaign for the Protection of Rural England was horrified at the urban sprawl swallowing up farmland. In 1933 it began to promote the idea of a 'Green Girdle' round London. Its campaign bore fruit in 1935 in the Restriction of Ribbon Development Act. The 'Girdle' eventually became the Green Belt.

Tackling road safety

Road deaths had become a 'hideous and growing blot on our national life', Oliver Stanley, the minister of transport, said in 1934. Upwards of 7,000 people a year

BRAVE NEW HOUSING

Conditions for those lucky enough to be rehoused improved sharply in the Thirties. This new flat (left) is part of a development built by the Bethnal Green and East London Housing Association at Brunswick Street, Hackney, in 1936. The wide balconies were set back from those on the floor below, to give them sun, forming a terraced pyramid shape. Flower boxes were incorporated in the design. Work is under way below on the Quarry Hill Flats pioneered by Leeds City Council. In 1939 this was one of the largest developments of flats in the world. Two thousand houses had been torn down in an area long classed as slums to create 938 new flats at a cost of £1.5 million. Feelings were mixed, though, on the merits of flats versus houses. Houses had a privacy and identity that was lost in high-rise development. The Quarry Hill flats were demolished in 1978.

were being killed, and tens of thousands injured. Some cottages near dangerous crossroads in the country were said to have become 'unofficial dressing stations', so many crashes took place near them, particularly at weekends. In large towns, the frequent fogs made worse by coal fires led to sudden spikes in accidents. Some local councils had already built pedestrian bridges to protect children at vulnerable spots, often over tram lines near schools. Now, Stanley began a sweeping safety campaign. New road signs – Major Road Ahead, One-Way Street, Roundabout – were brought in. White lines were painted on roads to delineate traffic lanes. Cyclists had to fix reflectors to rear mudguards. Leslie Hore-Belisha, who took over as transport minister later in 1934, gave his name to the orange beacons that were now installed on pedestrian crossings.

A 30mph speed limit was introduced in built-up areas. There was no limit elsewhere, just a general regulation against 'driving to the public danger'. It became compulsory to dip headlights when cars passed one another. Cars had to be fitted with windscreen wipers and splinter-proof windscreens. Hore-Belisha also introduced 'silence zones' in cities at night, where drivers were forbidden to use their horns. The active Anti-Noise League lobbied successfully to get silencers fitted to pneumatic road-drills. 'Courtesy cops' were equipped with loudspeakers

in their patrol cars, their voices booming down the road as they pulled people over to advise them how to drive better. Hore-Belisha also made a driving test compulsory and brought in driving examiners to administer it.

As a result of all these measures the annual death rate fell, but only to around 6,500 – in total, about 120,000 people were killed on the roads between the wars, and well over a million were injured. But at least the accident rate stayed flat, despite an ever-growing volume of traffic. As the number of car owners reached 2 million, taking a Sunday afternoon or Bank Holiday drive became a ritual. Cars were joined by charabancs, long-distance coaches, which were cheaper and more flexible than trains, and were soon used by sports fans and day trippers.

One development the British did not adopt was the motorway. Hitler had started building *autobahnen* in Germany when he came to power. They provided thousands of construction jobs, as well as giving a dramatic boost to traffic flows. They also separated fast-moving cars from the horses and carts, cyclists and pedestrians found even on major roads. The Automobile Association was invited in 1937 to send a delegation to Germany by Dr Fritz Todt, the Inspector General

HELPING HAND
Children are helped across the road in Cardiff. With road deaths well in excess of 7,000 a year, politicians in the Thirties felt something had to be done. In 1934 a new transport minister, Leslie Hore-Belisha, introduced the striped pole topped with an orange globe that still bears his name. Installed at road crossings like this one (above), Belisha beacons made it safer for pedestrians to cross the road. The sweeping road safety campaign of the Thirties also saw the introduction of a 30mph speed limit in built-up areas and the first compulsory tests for drivers assessed by driving examiners.

of German Roadways and the driving force behind the autobahnen. MPs and county surveyors joined AA officials to see the new roads first hand. The AA concluded that British needs were best met by improving existing roads rather than building brand-new high-speed routes across the countryside. Britain had to wait more than 20 years for its first modest motorway. For now, the East Lancs road linking Liverpool to Manchester was the extent of innovation. George V opened the road and the new Mersey road tunnel connecting Liverpool to the Wirral – the longest road tunnel in the world at the time – on 18 July, 1934.

NEWS FROM EUROPE

The big Continental story at the start of 1938 was the baby expected by Princess Juliana of the Netherlands. If it was a girl, Holland might be ruled by a succession of Queens for a century. It was a girl, too, born on 30 January.

In March, though, German troops upstaged Juliana as they marched unopposed into Austria. This was the 'Anschluss' in which Austria was annexed as a province of the German Reich. Britain did no more than send a protest note. Churchill demanded a grand alliance to stand against it. Prime Minister Chamberlain said that was impractical. For good measure, he gave the chairman of John Lewis's department store a 'high-powered rocket' for boycotting German goods.

'Horrible! Horrible! I never thought they would do it.'
Lord Halifax, Foreign Secretary, on Germany's annexation of Austria

Chamberlain did, though, accelerate Britain's rearmament. The recovery was well underway by now. Rearmament, with its demands for armour plate, explosives, ships, chemicals, uniforms, helped to breathe life back into the most depressed regions. The output of cars had doubled over five years. Electrical engineering was flourishing and now shipbuilding and steelmaking were transformed. Shares on the London Stock Exchange doubled. Robert Graves recorded a string of healthy economic signs on the front page of a single edition of the *Financial News* on 10 March, 1938: 'English Steel pay 20 per cent ... Cammell Laird (shipbuilding) Income Rises Sharply ... Royal Mail Lines Pay More ... Dunlop Pays 9 per cent ... Stock Exchange More Confident.'

Hitler's next move

Czechoslovakia had been created by the Treaty of Versailles in 1919, an artificial country made up of Bohemia and Slovakia, with 3 million German-speakers caught up in it in the Sudetenland. Hitler vowed that these 'Sudeten Deutsch' belonged to Germany and that he would see them incorporated in the Reich.

Chamberlain flew to meet Hitler at Godesberg, a pretty little town on the Rhine, on 14 September, 1938. Hitler at first proposed partitioning the Czech state, but then demanded that the Sudentenland must be wholly occupied by German troops. It was, he claimed, the 'last territorial demand I have to make in Europe'. On 24 September, Britain and France – and the Czechs – rejected the proposal. Chamberlain said that if France declared war on Germany, Britain

would support her. On 27 September, the Fleet was mustered, along with volunteer pilots and airmen of the Auxiliary Air Force. Europe was on the brink of war. The same day, the Queen launched the liner *Queen Elizabeth* in Glasgow.

Meeting at Munich

The British, French and Italian leaders met Hitler in Munich at the end of September. The Czechs and their Soviet allies were not invited. When Chamberlain was given 'Heil Hitler' salutes, he doffed his bowler hat in response. On his arrival, he mistook Hitler for a footman. He was only prevented from handing him his hat and coat by a desperate whisper from Ribbentrop.

Chamberlain knew what Hitler thought of the British well enough. Hitler, he said, contrasted the bitter struggle he had gone through in getting to power with the British, who were still living in their own little world, clinging to ineffective shibboleths like 'collective security', 'disarmament' and 'non-aggression pacts'. He was right – but he himself continued to hang onto the shibboleth of appeasement. The British ambassador in Berlin, Sir Neville Henderson, 'dapper, snobbish', said that the British would ultimately have to allow self-determination to the Austrians and Sudeten Germans under 'suitable guarantees', though he should have known by now that guarantees signed by Hitler were as valuable as so much wastepaper. It was agreed that German troops would occupy the Sudetenland on 1 October, with the frontiers to be settled by a Four Power commission after a plebiscite.

HONOURED GUEST
Neville Chamberlain is met by a guard of honour on arrival at Oberwiesenfeld airport in Munich in September 1938 (above). The Prime Minister was on his way for talks with Adolf Hitler to discuss German threats to invade Czechoslovakia. He was met by Nazi officials in brown uniforms and a senior SS officer, Obergruppenführer Ritter von Epp (on the far left, dressed in black). During their talks on the Czech crisis, Hitler and Chamberlain dined together (top right). Hitler's interpreter, Paul Schmidt, is second from right with the British ambassador to Germany, Neville Henderson, on the right. The picture was taken by Heinrich Hoffman, Hitler's favourite photographer. Meanwhile, back in Britain, trenches were being hastily dug in London parks against air raids, and loudspeaker appeals were made in cinemas and at sports events for people to hurry to have their gas masks fitted.

ICONIC MOMENT
Chamberlain after landing at Heston airport on his flight back from Munich (left). He waves a piece of paper, an agreement signed by Hitler that the return of the Sudetenland to Germany was the last of his territorial demands. Chamberlain told a relieved and happy crowd that this meant 'peace in our time'. It seemed a triumph for appeasement. 'I have no doubt, looking back, that my visit alone prevented an invasion for which everything was prepared', Chamberlain claimed. It did not. The Munich agreement doomed the Czechs, and merely postponed the war for eleven months.

Short-lived cheers

Before he left Munich to fly back to London, Chamberlain managed to persuade Hitler to sign a short declaration he had typed out. It declared the 'desire of our two peoples never to go to war with one another again'. It was this piece of paper that Chamberlain famously waved as he arrived to cheering crowds at Heston aiport. 'It is peace for our time', he declared. Large crowds cheered him when he appeared on the floodlit balcony with the King and Queen at Buckingham Palace that evening. They sang 'For he's a jolly good fellow'. Women cried 'Thank you, thank you' in tears of joy. London's West End filled with rejoicing people, bringing traffic to a standstill. Chamberlain was compared to a 'fairy prince' in one paper. The Swedes gave him a trout stream and the French named streets for him. 'We have looked squarely in the face of evil', the *Sunday Pictorial* assured its readers. 'And we have seen it vanish.'

LIFE GOES ON

Evil had not vanished, but for the great British public there was little to be done for now. The cinema was an escape from a still-dangerous world. Britain had about 5,000 cinemas by 1939 and some 20 million tickets were being sold each week. Some of the new 'Super Cinemas' could seat 4,000 filmgoers. The cinema was cheap – six pence a ticket for a show lasting two or three hours, with two films, a newsreel and perhaps a cartoon or 'short'. The cost was no more than a pint of beer, and it was even less at the 'penny pictures' on Saturday morning matinees.

It was just within reach of the unemployed, who often went a few times a week. Women could go on their own, unlike the pub, and of course courting couples appreciated the darkness. The lavish decor, thick carpets and deeply cushioned seats brought a touch of colour and extravagance to dreary lives.

The seven cinemas in York had a weekly audience in 1936 of 45,000, half the city's population. This was a growth business. By 1939, the city had ten cinemas and audiences were over 50,000 a week. Nevertheless, the coming of the 'talkies' at the start of the decade had been a disaster for thousands of cinema musicians. The big cinemas had employed orchestras to play throughout each performance, but with sound, they went the way of sub-titles.

The British film industry had some protection from Hollywood. By 1935, 20 per cent of films shown had to be British. The influx of refugees from the Continent helped. The Hungarian Korda brothers were behind hit costume dramas like *The Private Life of Henry VIII* in 1933, *The Scarlet Pimpernel* in 1934 and *The Four Feathers* in 1939. Alfred Hitchcock was the best British director, and though inevitably he went to Hollywood, he also made fine films at home, like *A Lady Vanishes* and *The Thirty-Nine Steps*. The official film censor,

BRITISH STARS
Robert Donat was one of the stars who drew worldwide audiences for British films. He won the 1939 Best Actor Oscar for his role in *Goodbye Mr Chips!*, beating Clark Gable and stopping *Gone with the Wind* from winning a clean sweep. Donat's first great hit was in *The Private Life of Henry VIII*, produced by Alexander Korda, a Hungarian who had come to Britain and founded the London Film Production and Denham Studios. Much of Britain's finest talent, though, drifted to Hollywood, including Charles Laughton, Vivien Leigh, Leslie Howard and Alfred Hitchcock.

REGULAR FILM-GOERS
The enraptured audience at a children's matinee performance. By 1939, there were almost 5,000 cinemas in Britain – Bolton alone, a town of 180,000 people, had 14. A survey in Liverpool in 1937 found that 40 per cent of people went to the cinema at least once a week, and one in four went twice a week or more.

Major Harding de Fonblanque Cox, was aged 81 and suffered from a type of lethargica that made him fall asleep when anything was put in front of him to read. 'Let us show clean films in the old country', he told the *Sunday Express*. 'I shall judge film stories as I would horse flesh or a dog. I shall look for clean lines.'

British documentary makers led the world with films sponsored by the Empire Marketing Board and the GPO film unit. Harry Watt's *Night Mail* in 1936 was a classic. A main aim of the British Film Institute, founded in 1933, was to encourage educational films. Fine films on natural history, on subjects like *The Tawny Owl* and *Rock Pools*, were made by Gaumont British Instructional.

Dance halls were the only real rival for a night out at the cinema and the pub. The Hammersmith Palais de Danse, which opened in 1919, was the archetype. By the Thirties, dance halls were nationwide. The BBC gave dancing a big boost, with the bandleaders Jack Payne and Henry Hall attracting huge followings, and a regular nightly slot for one of the big dance bands. 'Tea dances' in the mid-afternoon were popular with women and the unemployed. In 1930, Rochdale, with a population of around 100,000, had half a dozen dance venues open on Saturday nights, with admission charged between one and two shillings.

Another sort of dance, the ballet, was also having a good run. Ninette de Valois and Frederick Ashton were pioneers. Ralph Vaughan Williams' ballet *Job* opened a new composing direction for him. He and William Walton wrote film music, too. Arthur Bliss and Constant Lambert wrote music for new ballets. The dancer and teacher Marie Rambert's Ballet Club, with Ashton as choreographer, evolved into the Ballet Rambert. Robert Helpmann and Margot Fonteyn were the rising ballet stars in 1939. In opera, Glyndebourne had been founded in 1934.

Facing the music

Munich changed nothing. Duff Cooper, First Lord of the Admiralty since 1937, realised this and resigned in protest. *The Week* said that Chamberlain had 'turned all four cheeks to Hitler'. Prague was a 'city of sorrow', British correspondents reported, where solemn crowds gathered to shout: 'We want the whole Republic! We want to fight!' And the Germans were not the only ones with designs on Czech territory: the Poles demanded that areas inhabited by Poles be returned to them. Europe was turning cannibal. Italians listening to a speech by Count Ciano, their foreign minister, began screaming for 'Corsica, Nice, Tunisia, Djibouti'.

Hitler made a speech on 30 January, 1939, demanding the return of lost German colonies. These were far distant, in Africa. It was not, Chamberlain told himself and the nation, the 'speech of a man who is preparing to throw Europe into another crisis'. But Hitler was laying the foundations of his 'Thousand Year Reich'. On 15 March, 1939, his troops occupied the rest of Czechoslovakia. He did not stop with Prague. The former German city of Memel, a part of Lithuania since Versailles, was surrendered to him after an ultimatum on 22 March.

At last, Chamberlain began to fret that his trust in Hitler was misplaced. 'Is this an attempt to dominate the world by force?' he asked. It was, but Hore-Belisha warned of how little there was to stop him. He wanted a British Expeditionary Force of 19 divisions to be prepared to land in France. Only two were ready for service.

The Spanish war was over. Franco had broken through the half-starved Catalan army. Tens of thousands fled over the border to camps in France. In March, the Republican cabinet fled from Madrid and the great city surrendered. The Fascist successes emboldened Mussolini. On 5 April, without warning, the Italians began bombing Albanian towns. Three days later, organised resistance was over. King Zog fled, and began his long exile in Britain. Refugees came in growing numbers. In front of Hitler, Malcolm Muggeridge thought, they were like rabbits faced with the harvester. They gathered in the last corner of Western Europe where the scythe had not reached, where Parliament and books were still unburnt, letters of credit were still valid, the restaurants buzzed with chatter uninhibited by the fear of the secret police, where 'butter was still more evident than guns'.

> 'In spite of the hardness and ruthlessness I thought I saw in his face, I got the impression that here was a man who could be relied upon when he had given his word.'
>
> Prime Minister Neville Chamberlain on Hitler

THE SPANISH CIVIL WAR

Members of a British ambulance unit on the Tardiente Front in the Spanish Civil War in September 1936 (above). The Republican cause was already attracting British volunteers, some as front-line soldiers rather than medical staff. Stalin was arming the Republicans, and sending them Soviet artillerymen and other specialists. Mussolini and Hitler were doing the same for Franco's Fascists, even supplying bomber squadrons. The fact that the dictators had taken sides persuaded the British and French governments to remain neutral, to the fury of the Left. When the Basque and Asturias provinces fell to Franco, some 4,000 Basque children like this little girl (left) were given sanctuary near Southampton. The Right denounced them as 'Red hooligans' likely to 'corrupt our pure English youth', Robert Graves observed, whilst 'the Left defended them with aggressive sentimental pity'.

In all, more than 2,300 volunteers from Britain and Ireland joined the International Brigades to fight on the Republican side in Spain: 500 were killed. In December 1938, with Franco on the verge of victory, the last 305 British volunteers left by train. Clement Attlee, leader of the Labour Party, was among the crowd who welcomed them at Victoria Station. The fight against fascism was about to get a lot bigger.

FLEEING TO SAFETY
On 12 December, 1938, 502 child refugees from Vienna arrived at Harwich (left) to be taken by special train to Pakefield Holiday Camp at Lowestoft. Four hundred were Jewish, the others were 'non-Aryan' Catholics or Protestants, or the children of anti-Nazis. The occupation of Austria in March 1938, which had led them to flee, had been the first violent act of Nazi aggression outside Germany itself. It was a portent of disasters to come.

THE BALLOON GOES UP
A crowd in Downing Street read newspapers on the German invasion of Poland, while waiting to hear the British declaration of war. Until now, the press had tried to lighten the air of crisis, with stories like the arrival of the first giant panda at London Zoo. Behind the scenes, though, the government had already been making preparations for war. Rearmament was proceeding apace, air raid precautions were overhauled, and plans were well advanced for the evacuation of children from dangerous areas.

Some 25,000 refugees had arrived in Britain from Germany and Austria by 1939. Britain was traditionally an asylum for the persecuted – Karl Marx and Vladimir Lenin included – and many brought their jobs with them. German Jews brought the Leipzig fur trade, for example, and others set up tailoring and furnishings factories. Sigmund Freud arrived from Vienna in January 1938.

Hitler next turned on the Poles. He wanted to recover the Polish territory that separated East Prussia from eastern Germany. This was called the 'Polish corridor' and it included the port of Danzig. Stalin offered to send Soviet troops to guard against the German threat. The Poles, who had suffered Russian rule before, declined the offer. Under the Germans, they said, they would lose their freedom. The Soviets would take their souls. On 23 August, 1939, to the immense surprise of all but the dictators themselves, the Nazis and Communists signed a non-aggression pact. It had a secret clause: the two would share Poland between them.

In Britain, the violence in the last days of peace came not from the Continent but from the IRA. Eamonn de Valera had made Eire a republic, but the IRA would not accept continued British rule in the north. They began a campaign in England to pressure the British to abandon Ulster. Time bombs were planted in left-luggage offices. On 25 August, 1939, an IRA bomb in Coventry killed 25 people.

German troops invaded Poland from the west on 1 September. The Soviets would attack from the east a little later. On 3 September, Britain and France declared war on Germany. What followed was aptly called the Phoney War. In the last months of the Thirties, the blackout caused more British deaths than any fighting. The cities were dark, and London was almost childless as evacuation got under way. The blackout was blamed for 1,130 casualties. The Navy had 586, the RAF 79, the Army none. But all too real a war was waiting in the wings.

ON THE BRINK OF THE WAR

For most of the Thirties, with memories of the Great War still raw in people's minds, Britain's politicians did all they could to avoid involvement in another war. And the public applauded them for doing so. But at the end of the decade, practically everyone accepted that a stand must be made against Hitler and Nazi Germany. When the declaration of war came, people calmly accepted the situation and carried on – after making sure that as many children as possible were evacuated out of harm's way from the cities to the country. There they would be safe from the German bombers that people knew would make the Second World War more terrifying by far for civilians than the First.

CHILDREN AT WAR
Children on the beach at Whitley Bay in Northumberland (now Tyne and Wear) help to fill sandbags to protect local buildings and shelters (left). More than a million children like these young boys with name tags and gas masks (right), as well as mothers and babies, were evacuated from cities in September 1939. In the cities they left behind, posters in the Air Raid Precaution campaign urged people to volunteer to help save lives and property in bombing raids (above). Many evacuees came from the poorest and most overcrowded slums of the big cities. Their condition often shocked the middle-class and country people who housed them. The children had head-lice, impetigo and scabies, and they were often unwashed. Some had no change of clothes – 'house-holders had to keep the children in bed while they washed their clothes', a report found – while others arrived in garments so verminous they had to be burnt. 'Some children arrived sewn into a piece of calico with a coat on top and no other clothes at all.' The social shock waves caused by the evacuees stirred the national conscience.

A message painted on a pavement (below) in Chorlton, Manchester, reminds everyone to carry their gas mask. In the event, poison gas was never used during the war. Women right), 'somewhere in England', on 21 September, 1939, as the men marched off to war. And a family try out their new air raid shelter on hearing the air raid warning (bottom right). The fighting were to be terrible indeed, but they had not come yet. The Thirties ended in the Phoney War, with aircraft dropping propaganda leaflets, not bombs, and the troops of in France doing little more than training exercises. Only in the war at sea, against the U-boats, was there real ferocity. All that would change, brutally and utterly, in May 1940.

'This is a sad day for all of us …
I trust I may live to see the day when
Hitlerism has been destroyed and a
liberated Europe … re-established.'

Prime Minister Neville Chamberlain, 3 September, 1939

INDEX

PICTURE ACKNOWLEDGEMENTS

Abbreviations: t = top; m = middle; b = bottom; r = right; c = centre; l = left

All images in this book are courtesy of Getty Images, including the following which have additional attributions:
8, 16, 21, 22-3, 32l, 64b, 76, 78, 81, 90, 91b, 102t, 104, 106, 116, 117b, 122, 127tl, 135, 140, 151, 152-3: Popperfoto
10, 146, 155: Time & Life Pictures
28, 30, 33, 37, 59: Imagno
48l, 49: Felix Man/Getty Images
88t: Lytton Strachey/Getty Images

LOOKING BACK AT BRITAIN
DEPRESSION YEARS – 1930s
is published by The Reader's Digest Association Ltd, London, in association with Getty Images and Endeavour London Ltd.

Copyright © 2010 The Reader's Digest Association Ltd

The Reader's Digest Association Ltd
11 Westferry Circus
Canary Wharf
London E14 4HE
www.readersdigest.co.uk

Endeavour London Ltd
21–31 Woodfield Road
London W9 2BA
info@endeavourlondon.com

Written by
Brian Moynahan

For Endeavour
Publisher: Charles Merullo
Designer: Tea Aganovic
Picture editors: Jennifer Jeffrey, Franziska Payer Crockett
Production: Mary Osborne

For Reader's Digest
Project editor: Christine Noble
Art editor: Conorde Clarke
Indexer: Marie Lorimer
Proofreader: Ron Pankhurst
Pre-press account manager: Dean Russell
Product production manager: Claudette Bramble
Production controller: Sandra Fuller

Reader's Digest General Books
Editorial director: Julian Browne
Art director: Anne-Marie Bulat

Colour origination by Chroma Graphics Ltd, Singapore
Printed and bound in China

We are committed both to the quality of our products and the service we provide to our customers. We value your comments, so please do contact us on 08705 113366 or via our website at
www.readersdigest.co.uk

If you have any comments or suggestions about the content of our books, email us at
gbeditorial@readersdigest.co.uk

CONCEPT CODE: UK 0154/L/S
BOOK CODE: 638-011 UP0000-1
ISBN: 978 0 276 44399 2
ORACLE CODE: 356900011H.00.24